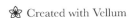 Created with Vellum

PRAISE FOR HALF MY SKY

"Carrie's writing is visceral, soul-bearing, and absolutely vital for propelling us towards a more inclusive and compassionate society. She unapologetically challenges and dismantles ableism at its very core."
Sophia San Filippo, Love What Matters

"Reading Carrie's stories about Jack has been an important part of my autism education over the years. Carrie describes perfectly the emotional rollercoaster she experiences, one that many parents will be able to relate to. Half My Sky documents Jack's journey into adulthood, a future that was once so scary and far off, that is now all so real and full of possibilities. An essential read for any autism family."
James Hunt, Stories About Autism

"Half My Sky has been transformative for me. Carrie's journey with Jack is so relatable, nothing short of inspiring, and comes at a pivotal moment in my parenting journey. The perspective shift from "letting go" to "untethering" was something I desperately needed. It now serves as a guiding light that's helping me to allow my three autistic children the necessary space to grow and learn independently as they explore their teen and young adult years."
Rob Gorski, The Autism Dad

"Through a series of heartwarming, authentic, witty and vulnerable letters, *Half My Sky* is a reflection on the realities and sometimes messiness that defines family life, particularly when adding an autism diagnosis to the mix. Carrie's desire for her son Jack to have a meaningful adulthood full of joy and independence is a relatable feeling for any mother. However, learning to let them go is the toughest part."
- Laurie Hellmann, author of *Welcome to My Life: A Personal Parenting Journey Through Autism*, and host of *Living the Sky Life* podcast

Praise From Followers

"Carrie has paved the way for those of us behind her on our own journey with our amazing kids."
Kelli Bright Whitlock

"Carrie Cariello's writing gives me confidence to dare to dream about my family's future after my own son's autism diagnosis. Her words are like a warm hug from a dear friend. 'Half my sky' is both relatable and inspiring."
Jodi Claus

"Carrie Cariello's story reaches beyond those touched by autism. Her stories and life lessons relate to all of us in some way."
Kathey McEachin

"I remember a story Carrie told about the time Jack was in a grocery store, and about the look on a young girls face before and after recognizing that Jack was different. I will forever be aware of my reaction, and interaction with people with disabilities because of her stories. She has a gift of bringing her readers into her, and her family's world."
Linda Quirion Lessard

"As a grandmother of an autistic 7-year old girl, I have learned so much from Carrie over the last two years! Carrie has a way with words and a sparkly personality to go with it. She carries the heaviness of the autism world with much grace and dignity, and you can truly see how much she loves her family. Her heart and soul are very apparent in this book."
Janet E Carr

"Carrie's words resonate in me in ways I have felt all along but could not put into words. Raw yet compassionate and makes me feel we are not alone."

Claire Phelan Holloway

"Half My Sky is an honest and vulnerable story of a how one mother found a loving way to help her son find his independence in a world full of round edges that didn't fit his unbending corners."

Jennifer Boyd Ross

"By sharing her family's journey, Carrie has helped countless others realize what can be possible in the coming years. Every one of us can relate to something we see in this boy named Jack. Her words are comforting to those of us with neurodiverse children, and insightful to those with typical children. And through her stories, we can all hold more space for those who walk a different path and honor the importance they add to this world."

Jessica Sellitti Ayari

"You have given us such hope for our grandson. Your vulnerable story gives families such hope in developing a plan long term for their children."

Lynn Lynch

"Carrie's writing and love for her family is good for my autism mom heart. I look forward to her writing and live videos to help my family navigate this messy world with our 18-year old son."

Jennie Jeter Trueblood

"Carrie has so eloquently shared her family through the hard, exhausting, messy, and joyous beauty this life is. She exudes hope and inspiration to all moms and families who at times can only see darkness. Jack is an inspiration and I, like so many of Carrie's followers are so very proud of the man he has become."

Ka Tie

"Carrie does not waste a single word. Her ability to choose the exact words that complement her story are a testament to how we all relate to the Cariello family."

Randy Allen

"Carrie Cariello's poignant storytelling helps me remember that I am not alone in my journey as a mom in discovering who we are as a family and what we each need to keep moving forward, together."

Debra Majeske

"Carrie's words always pull at my heartstrings. I find answers to questions I didn't know I had in her writings. The look we are privileged to have into her family is a gift."

Lisa Ingold

Half My Sky

Autism, Marriage, and the
Messiness that is Building a Family.

Carrie Cariello

To the man
whose hand I clasped
when you were little more than a boy.

I loved you the very first day
on a campus bright with sunlight
as autumn's confetti crunched beneath our feet.

Through fire and autism and breathlessness and air.
I love you still.
I love you still.

You hold up half my sky.

CONTENTS

INTRODUCTION

I am told the average human heart weighs less than a pound. It is considered to be the hardest-working muscle in the body. It beats approximately 115,000 times daily, carrying oxygen and the food, vitamins, and minerals our body needs to move, think, grow, and heal.

A heart song, on the other hand, is a story. It is the tiny heartbreaks behind the muscle – the by-product of building a family.

My story is not a new story. For the longest time, I thought it started with a boy. Now, I am less sure.

Hi.

My name is Carrie.

I am married to a man named Joe. We have five kids. Our second son, Jack, is diagnosed with autism.

I am writing this introduction as I begin the prep for a colonoscopy. It seems a fitting metaphor, even if I can't quite decide how.

The phone on my battery is low. My laptop felt too cumbersome to lug upstairs and arrange where I sit on the bed, so I've turned to old-fashioned pen and paper.

This afternoon, I met with my editor. A few days ago, I emailed her suggesting a change of plans for this book; I want to write it as a series of letters.

"Why letters?" she asked through the computer screen. Holiday lights twinkled in the background of her home office.

Sitting at my desk, I squinted at the pictures I hung on the walls some years ago – white trees my daughter painted, a blue penguin by my youngest son, Henry. I pondered her question.

She's very nice, my editor. She mostly lets me do my own thing. I submit chapters at my own pace, navigating the content that feels most precious to me and discarding the rest. But she was concerned, perhaps rightfully so, when I suddenly changed course nearly halfway through, suggesting we rework things a bit.

"Because," I answered. "I am terrible at writing chapters."

It's true. To me, *chapters* feel too much like reporting – the laying out of information and timelines. And if there's anything that defies reporting, it's the magical slippery riddle that is building a family around autism.

For eighteen years, I have looked at autism from every angle I could imagine. Holding it up like a prism, I consider the smooth planes, the sharp edges, and the occasional bursts of color during bouts of gray.

I saw it through my children's eyes, our community's glances, and the stares of strangers.

How it affected my marriage, my friendships, and my son himself.

An introduction is supposed to provide a roadmap for the reader – a framework intended to announce the cast of characters inside the narrative.

Yet there is little framework to contain the musings of the heart or the music between the beats of ordinary life. Pork chops on white plates, arguments over hats in winter, bikes left out in the rain.

As for the cast of characters, Joe and I got married when I was one month shy of twenty-four. Like most things in life, I embarked upon marriage before truly understanding why – or what it meant. Looking back, it would have been impossible to comprehend the enormity that is intertwining one's life with another person.

Four years later, our first son was born. We named him Joseph.

Thirteen months after Joseph, along came another boy. We named him John but called him Jack. Little did we know that this John/Jack would forever alter the course of our lives.

Enamored by new motherhood, we quickly had more children until one day, we had a house of toddlers and infants, all grasping hands and tiny, beckoning voices.

Charlie, the dark-haired boy with chocolate eyes.

Rose, my autism whisperer, my canary in the mine, my daughter with curly hair and a thoughtful gaze.

And Henry, the fifth, the final, the youngest child born with a fierce determination to be first at everything.

I love them the way the thirsty earth loves the rain. Yet, at times, I am overwhelmed and uncertain. Growing humans doesn't always come naturally to me. I yell about stupid stuff.

When Jack was eighteen months old, he was diagnosed with autism. We were expecting it. We were prepared. Except we were precisely the opposite.

Over time, this diagnosis became the lens through which I view life's details.

I go through the security line in an airport and wonder if Jack could ever manage it on his own.

I pass a teenager bouncing a basketball on the sidewalk, and I think of all the ways in which autism has stolen my son's ease.

Even something as benign as a colonoscopy prep calls to mind my own mortality. What if the doctor, all blue scrubs and solemn face, comes into the room tomorrow to deliver unthinkable news? Who will take care of them – of him? Who will buy his favorite birthday cake and chase down his monthly medication?

From there, it's a short leap to Jack in his twenties, his thirties, and beyond.

Who will continue to explain boy to world and world to boy?

I can't die.

This is the mantra of every special-needs mother.

We can't die.

Yet immortality belongs to no one.

This is why I tell our story.

I've told it even when people warned me not to share.

I've told it when I didn't think it would mean anything to anyone.

I've told it as an insurance of sorts, hoping against all hope someone will pick up the baton and carry it when I no longer can.

After all, if compassion is a house we build, then storytelling is the key to the front door.

This book is everything I've ever wanted to say out loud if only I'd been brave or quick or thoughtful enough in the moment. It is a place to confess what was once hard to admit; building a family is a messy business.

Tonight, I drink my prep liquid and smell the dinner my husband and our youngest son prepare together, below me in the kitchen. Maybe they will save me some. For tomorrow.

This book is mine, and it is also yours. I offer it to you with palms outstretched. Take from it what you like – what you need.

Solace, comfort, hard-won advice. Hope.

Dear reader, welcome to our house.

1

ORDINARY SPARKLE

DEAREST MAMA.

Tender Father.

I know. Today was the day you dreaded and feared.

Diagnosis day always brings us up short. We're not made for it. No one is.

Even those more prepared – those of us who had the words circling the back of our minds like wispy smoke at a campfire – well, our knees still buckle at the formal announcement. How could they not?

Autism Spectrum Disorder.

The next day, we try to return to our ordinary lives because life goes on even though we hate it.

We make breakfast. We buy fabric softener. We load the dishwasher, run errands, and generally grit our teeth through it all.

Yet there is a strange, tender period between the diagnosis and the new life part.

The telling.

Now, you have to tell people.

Family, coworkers, friends, neighbors.

Teachers, babysitters, cousins.

The ladies at church, the librarian, the pharmacist.

This is very, very hard work. It is the kind of work that makes you feel naked, exposed, and wholly unprepared.

We try to decide how – and when? A phone call? An email? During Christmas dinner? Or Easter brunch?

How can we tell something we hardly understand ourselves?

Autism. What does it mean? What will it change?

Nothing. Everything.

Instead, we stay quiet. For now, this is our secret to clasp between our palms. There will be plenty of time to tell what they may already know.

Our minds flit to the future – proverbial moths to the flame – then shrink back before we feel the burn.

We think briefly about the books we devoured about parenting, earmarked on shelves for future reference. Topics like how to raise a well-adjusted child, when to give the sex talk, and where to draw the line on curfews all ring hollow, for we are about to embark on a journey for which there is no manual.

After all, what do you reference when the future has so drastically changed?

We consider other children and all that will change for them.

Autism is a loudly ticking clock. From the moment the diagnosis is delivered – for some of us, it happens way before the officialness of the office and the forms and the words – we feel the seconds and minutes whizzing by at shocking speeds.

So, we reduce. We turn to metrics.

Age.

Dates.

Numbers.

It was November 2006.

He was eighteen months old.

The appointment was at 10:30 in the morning.

Slowly, we add color to the landscape. Color smooths out the edges. It softens even the harshest words. Because an autism diagnosis is harsh, no matter how gentle the delivery.

I dressed him in overalls. Then I zipped up his blue jacket against the late-autumn chill.

We walked back to the car. The parking garage was mostly empty. I buckled him into his car seat. I think I kissed him on the cheek, but I can't remember. I drove back out into the afternoon. It started to rain, the clouds telling a story all their own.

It had all come down to a single moment. One single moment solidified the months of worry, the late-night conversations, the stares in the grocery store.

He slammed his shin on the corner of a filing cabinet. As I traded information with the young doctor in the tiny office, Jack whirled and spun. He was breathless yet silent. Then, all at once, he lost his balance and fell. As metal bit into skin, he dropped to the floor three feet from me and howled.

And the kindly doctor asked if this mysterious, curious, wild boy of mine ever came to me for comfort.

No. No, he did not.

Diagnosis day.

All at once, there is everything to do.

Yet nothing to be done.

Instead, we take stock. We consider the inventory.

He can stack two blocks together.

He slept three hours last night.

He tried one bite of banana before he spit it on the table.

We hold hope beneath our ribcage.

In some ways, hope is worse than the metrics.

Hope is more than dates and numbers blocks on the carpet. It is even brighter than color. It is fire and light. It is the bag of rocks we strap to our backs as we climb uphill.

With hope, we have so much to lose.

Years pass. We dream new dreams.

Instead of touchdowns on a field, we cheer for words during therapy.

Small to many, our triumphs are king-size to us.

Somewhere along the way, we learn how to tell.

And it turns out the telling part is good. There is a special healing beauty in it. Our voices get stronger each time. Our spirits feel braver.

The first person I told was a stranger. We were at the Bronx Zoo.

It was crowded and hot. Jack took every opportunity to run away from me.

When he wasn't running into crowds of people, he was trying to grab half-eaten pretzels from the garbage cans or snatch napkins off the hotdog carts.

He was terrified of the animals – all of them – the doe-eyed deer in their green valleys, the multicolored birds peering down from their perch. He screamed and banged his head every time we walked to a new display.

By the end of the afternoon, I was desperate. We were waiting in line for one last exhibit, and he squirmed, jumped, screeched – finally dropping to the ground, thrashing wildly. I picked him up like a potato sack under my arm while everyone stared.

I announced loudly that he had autism. And just like that, life snapped into focus.

My son has autism.

Over time, it became my salvation, my repentance, my battle cry, my gulp of fresh blue air, all wrapped up inside of four words.

When Jack was four, he had a hard time walking down the stairs. Carefully, he'd place one foot down, then step the other foot to meet it.

We invented a game to help him. We named it after the brightly colored plastic bricks. Side by side, we stood, showing him how to move a whole stair step at a time.

One Lego, two Lego, three Lego, four!

At night, I dreamed in color. I dreamed in plastic. I dreamed of long, winding staircases.

When he was eight, we watched The Wizard of Oz. As the credits rolled by at the end, he sat straight up and announced, "The Lion. He has autism."

I asked him why. Why would he think that?

"Because he is afraid. All the time."

That night, I dreamed of a lion's eyes, pleading and lost.

I have lived alongside autism for eighteen years now.

Still, I have moments when my breath catches.

Driving through town, I notice teenage boys with their easy smiles and calm limbs. I think of Jack, jumping and twitching his fingers, and my stomach drops.

I watch athletes on the basketball court during March Madness, and I wonder what might have become of my six-foot, five-inch son if autism hadn't commandeered his arms and legs like a puppeteer with a marionette.

It's true that autism is heartbreak by one thousand papercuts. Some sting nearly constantly. Others rear up and cut deep when we least expect it.

Dearest Mama.

Tender Father.

You will never forget this day, it's true.

Please. Do all the things I didn't do.

Cradle his head between your hands.

Bend down and smell his hair after a bath.

Share a cookie before dinner.

Notice.

Notice what he can do instead of what he can't.

Buy the balloon in the grocery store – the one that floats toward the ceiling, dusty and half-deflated.

Buy it because his eyes lit up when he saw it.

You see, my Jack is eighteen now.

When I wasn't looking, he grew up.

It feels as though we're in the end game, as he perches upon the precipice of manhood.

In a few months, he will head off to a residential program. He will audit one class a semester at a community college.

It's not about a degree. We could care less about a degree.

It's about an experience to call his own.

It's about life in a college setting where students order take-out and collect in common areas and belong to one another in the spirit of friendship.

We did the work. And the work landed us here – on the cusp of something bigger than we ever imagined.

It is scary business, launching a boy-Jack into a man-world.

I think about crosswalks, mean people, loneliness, homesickness, sexual predators, cyberbullies, and cold nights when the wind chill dips.

I think about the demands of academics at a college level and wonder if we didn't aim too high.

When you raise a neurotypical child, there is often a familiar trajectory. High school, college, girlfriend, wedding, career, family. These are good things. They are whole, and ordinary, and right.

When you raise a diagnosed child, you are forced to acknowledge a different narrative.

Guardianship, power of attorney, residential facilities, full-time support.

When a neurotypical child leaves the proverbial nest, you hope you have prepared him enough for the world.

With a diagnosed child, you hope you have prepared the world enough for him.

Still, nearly two decades after a parking garage, I keep metrics.

He can do laundry.

He can cook a meal.

He can pay for his soda with a debit card.

Can he make a friend?

Can he concentrate long enough to complete a paper?

Autism is a little like wearing glasses with two very different lenses.

When I look through one side, I see all the progress this boy has made. I see a high school senior when 6th grade was a disaster. I see the occasional small smile.

Yet the other lens tells a different story.

I can't imagine him sitting through a college class – listening to the lecture or taking notes. I can't imagine him interacting with a professor or turning in assignments.

I can't imagine him away from us.

Earnest Mama.

Hopeful Father.

Find each other.

You are partners first, parents second.

Love each other boldly. Fearlessly.

Please, dance before bedtime.

Turn up the music and clap to the beat.

You are going to make a mess of things some days. That's just how it goes.

Forgive yourself.

You are the mother. You are the father.

Resist the urge to be anything else: speech therapist, behavior analyst, teacher.

The work will always be there. That is the very thing about the work; it is the stray cat on the back step, begging for more attention and milk.

Think less about tomorrow and more about today.

Take off the glasses with the double lenses.

After all, childhood isn't measured in progress or years.

It is measured in moments.

It is moments full of delight and despair.

It is faded beach towels and stomach bugs and cannonballs on sunny afternoons.

It is winter snowballs, spring bike rides, and unexpected thunderstorms – all strung together like lights on a string.

Despite the diagnosis, we build a life. Somehow, some way, we do this.

The ordinary begins to sparkle. Warm toast with lots of butter. Brightly colored blocks towering in the air. Fresh sheets at the end of a long day. These very things keep the birds in the sky.

We look up and see the stars. We hear notes of music and smile. All is not lost. All is not gone. We've changed our address, and still, we find a way to walk home.

We have so much to lose.

Always, we hope.

There is no end game. There is simply healing and hurting and trying and building.

I love him fiercely.

My son.

My sun.

His favorite color is blue.

Dearest Mama.

Tender Father.

Cradle his head.

Inhale his dewy sweetness.

Feel the music in your tender, loose limbs and smile for the loveliness of this one and only life.

It's going to be okay.

2

BROKEN

I PULLED the door open and stepped inside the small, overheated vestibule.

For the second time that week, I nodded and smiled at the woman in the office. I filled out a name tag and made my way toward classroom 135 on the first floor.

The air felt charged.

A few people had walkie-talkies. Their expressions were serious, worried.

Kids stood lining the hallways. I thought maybe it was a fire drill.

As I got closer and closer to the classroom, I realized it was another kind of emergency altogether. A student was being unsafe. He was throwing things off his desk.

I reached the classroom door and nodded to the teacher. She stepped aside and gestured for me to enter the room.

A boy sat, huddled in the corner, his face in his hands. He was surrounded by textbooks. He sobbed big gulps of air. His cheeks were red and damp.

You.

My son.

Jack.

BORN IN BUFFALO, New York, you are the second of five kids. It was Mother's Day.

Even as an infant, there was a restlessness about you, as though you were uncomfortable in your own skin. You slept through the night at two weeks, then stopped again when you were around four months old. You'd wake, screaming and inconsolable.

Plagued by ear infections and a deep respiratory cough, we discovered you had reflux. We attempted medicine to soothe you, but at six months, you needed tubes in your ears and your adenoids removed.

The entire time, I had a pit beneath my ribcage that wouldn't go away. I felt like something was off – something I couldn't quite name.

You were my second baby in thirteen months, yet you couldn't have been more different from your older brother.

Joseph was engaging. He spoke early and laughed easily. He enjoyed games like patty-cake and itsy-bitsy spider.

In comparison, you often seemed checked out or detached. You stared vacantly when we called your name. Your language was slow to develop. You never pointed.

When it came time to introduce solid food, you had trouble managing it. It was as though you couldn't figure out how to use your tongue to push small bites of banana and cereal to the back of your mouth and swallow. Mealtimes turned into a disaster.

If you wanted something – juice, a DVD, a snack – you pulled us by the hand as a way of getting it.

Do you remember the house in Buffalo, Jack-a-boo? The small blue bedroom you shared with Joseph? The staircase where you used a black Sharpie to draw long, sweeping lines the week before we put it up for sale?

We made appointments. We talked to the pediatrician. We worked with a speech therapist to coax words from your lips.

We began to learn all the fancy terms for the vacancy and the hand-pulling.

Limited eye contact.

Lack of joint attention.

Self-directed.

And when you were eighteen months old, we learned the umbrella term for all of it: Autism Spectrum Disorder.

It was a cold day in November. The sky was spitting a metallic rain.

As we walked through the parking garage, your little hand in mine, I feverishly wished for a crystal ball.

What would you be like a year from now?

In kindergarten?

Fourth grade?

That's where my brain stopped.

I never imagined life beyond elementary school.

I never thought about whether you'd go to the prom, play a varsity sport, or drive a car.

I especially never thought about puberty.

YOU WERE twelve when your voice began to deepen, and your body started to change. You were in sixth grade.

Sixth grade was a very hard year – harder, even, than the toddler meltdowns and hearing the diagnosis or setting up all your services in elementary school.

In sixth grade, the entire social landscape changed.

I just love the phrase *social landscape.* It sounds lofty and important and smart. It suggests a backdrop where friends frolic and laugh, calling to mind sunny days and ice cream cones.

In reality, social landscape is the terrain upon which relationships are developed and sustained. Unfortunately, during middle school and adolescence, this terrain can be rocky. It shifts without warning, leaving one stranded – and often alone.

Most kids adapt to the changes after a while. Maybe they drift to a new group of friends or join a club they find interesting.

You aren't most kids. You are not known for your flexibility or ability to *drift*, if you will. You weren't interested in belonging to a club, no matter how many times we encouraged it.

"Hey, Jack, how about the chess club? They meet every – "

"No."

"Well, we could try swimm – "

"Nothing. For me."

An occupational therapist once told me younger children with autism are drawn to the company of girls because, at that stage of development, girls will handle most of the communication. In your case, this was true. Throughout elementary school, you often had a cluster of little girls who talked for you, sat with you at lunch, and helped you navigate the complicated land that is the playground.

The same therapist explained that as kids develop into tweens – those lovely pre-adolescent years between ages ten and thirteen – girls resort to *non-verbal social clues*, and then you are left in the dust of their eye rolls and shoulder shrugs.

For a little while, you had a group of boys you identified with and who engaged you with on the playground for short bouts of four square or tag. But you were unable to handle the fluidity of the friendships . . . and how one day there might be a new person playing while another wandered off to another game.

It enraged you.

In sixth grade, it was one of the warmest winters on record here in New Hampshire. Yet, through the long months of January and February, it snowed *inside* our house. Autism had unleashed a cold, harsh blizzard.

You became aggressive and depressed.

You stopped sleeping. All night long, I'd listen as you tossed and turned in your room down the hall. Every morning, I'd find your covers balled up at the foot of the bed.

You bit your fingernails until they bled. You picked a hole in your scalp. You were remote and far, far, away.

At school, you kicked. You bit. You screamed and cried and sobbed.

In your most panicked, frantic moment, you talked about knives and hurting yourself. We hid them once you went to bed at night. We were terrified.

Through it all, my mother's heart ached.

We asked you what was wrong. "Nothing. Everything."

We met with your team. "Jack seems to be struggling quite a bit with his peers."

You drew tombstones on white paper. You repeated phrases erratically.

In the evening, I made phone calls to mothers after you had lashed out at their sons and daughters. "I am terribly sorry about what he said today. My son is having a tough time. We are working on it."

EVERY NIGHT, Daddy and I sat up late. We turned options over and over – was this just puberty? Or another uptick in your ever-present anxiety? Were the academics too demanding? How much longer could it last?

Desperate, we turned to a neuropsychologist for an evaluation. Dr. G.

Week after week, after a quick stop at McDonald's for lunch, we trudged through the slushy parking lot and up one floor of a medical office, where you sat with the young dark-haired doctor for various tests. Some involved problem-solving concepts. Others, a test of working memory, emotional well-being, and language comprehension.

You liked her. You complied with the testing, albeit with a lot of breaks for snacks. But you cooperated.

My son, in life and motherhood, some details are easily forgotten. Others are hazy at first. They take a while to come into focus.

Yet meeting with the doctor to learn the results of your time together is still razor sharp. From the sound of a car starting in the parking lot below us to the panic spreading through my ribcage, I remember it all.

"Well," Dr. G. said gently, "He has some issues with working memory."

I looked at Joe and back at her. I nodded my head. I'd heard of working memory.

"Picture our working memory to be this entire table," she continued.

She spread her hands over the wood surface. "We have all this space to arrange our ideas." She fanned some of her papers out to demonstrate.

"We can organize the things we're thinking about. We can put some things here," she said, gesturing to the right.

"And other things here." She moved a folder to the left.

"But Jack, well, his working memory is more like this." She made a small circle with her hands in the empty corner of the table. "He doesn't really have as much."

You don't have much working memory. Your table is empty. Like a gust of wind on a rainy day, autism swept all your cerebral papers, folders, and Post-it notes to the floor.

"It's as if we all have a filing cabinet in our minds," she continued, stepping inside of my reverie. "It's where we store all the information we absorb throughout the day. Jack has his own kind of filing system, but it's hard to know what that's like. His information is, well, it seems complicated."

I uncrossed my legs and then crossed them again. I glanced at Daddy in the chair next to me. He seemed to be squinting at something on the wall.

"His cognitive thinking is quite impaired. He's at probably less than two percent of his peers at this point, but it's difficult to tell because his anxiety gets in the way."

"Based on his scores, his reading comprehension is close to that of a first grader."

"While I was testing him, he often said things like he feels like a loser – that he feels alone."

"When I showed him a math problem, he would tell me he's dumb at math, he can't do it."

I struggled to stay focused. I pictured you in first grade. You were so cute. I had bought you a red backpack for the first day of school, your name stitched across the front in white letters.

Jack.

"You see, he doesn't process language the same way we do. For Jack, listening to people talk all day is like you or I sitting in a

French class, except we don't speak French. He only understands bits and pieces here and there."

I remember feeling a powerful wave of regret and fear, like nausea. The room was hot.

"I do think he's probably a little depressed."

WHEN YOU HAVE an out-of-control child at school, the inclination is to discipline for bad days and reward for good ones.

Oftentimes, disciplining a child at 4:00 in the afternoon for an episode they had before lunch doesn't work. Some kids don't connect the dots that way. They don't fast-forward to a possible consequence and make a better choice.

Oftentimes, their behavior is not a choice.

Your behavior was not a choice.

You didn't choose the paralyzing anxiety that followed you everywhere you went.

You didn't choose to elevate your own nervous system to the point of complete deregulation.

You didn't choose to cry and sob while all your classmates looked on, bewildered and concerned.

Then, coated with a thin veneer of shame and embarrassment, you'd have to go back to school and face it all again.

"For Mom. Everyone saw me cry."

Much of the time – then and now – you live in what we call *fight* or *flight* mode. This is a state of acute stress when the body's nervous system becomes activated according to real *or perceived* fear.

At some point, we learned that you can only match the highest regulatory system in the room. If someone becomes elevated, your nervous system also climbs. The difference is that you are less able to bring it back down without assistance.

Every day after school, you'd walk in the door, drop your backpack, and immediately head upstairs. Without a word, you would climb into my bathtub. Fully clothed, without the water on, you'd lie there with your eyes closed and your arms straight down by your sides. Slowly, your limbs would relax. Watching you reminded me of a caterpillar in a cocoon.

The thing is, when you were little, your needs were so much more concrete and tangible. You didn't use words, so we bought picture books. We pointed to the apple and the banana and the monkey and the duck. We flapped our arms like a chicken and drew circles on paper with crayons.

Executive function, theory of mind, reading comprehension, isolation – they each disappear like vapor through my fingers; these fine, tenuous ghosts of his autism for which there are no pictures.

Nothing had prepared me for this point in motherhood – not a single article, book, or conversation. There is no how-to guide with instructions about easing a neurodiverse teenager through the storm of puberty. I only knew that what we were doing wasn't helping.

I decided to take my cues from you. Watching your face and limbs relax in the afternoon light of the bathtub, realized you didn't need me to ask why you shouted at the recess monitor again.

You didn't need me to nag you to pull out your homework, tell you to stop pacing the room, or remind you that we need to use nice words in school.

You didn't need us to threaten to take away your television time.

You needed a safe landing – a place where you could shut out the outside world with all of its confusing social structures and difficult demands . . . and simply breathe.

Home.

Frankly, we all needed it. As your emotional stability waxed and waned, our entire family felt like we were on a roller coaster right along with you. We desperately needed to slow the ride.

And that's what we did.

We developed a rhythm to our days – a framework to help shore the rising tide of autism's rage and chaos.

We lit candles during dinner. We sat beside one another in the soft glow and ate pork chops from white plates, followed by ice cream in Disney-themed bowls.

In the grocery store, I bought small treats I knew you enjoyed. Avocados. Golden Oreos. Pretzel rods.

At night, all seven of us sat in the living room and watched episodes of Scooby Doo, America's Got Talent, and Modern Family.

Every morning, I made your bed.

I pulled the sheets up tight, and I arranged the red and blue striped comforter on top. I folded the weighted blanket and tucked it into the bottom of the mattress.

It's corduroy, your weighted blanket. You never liked sleeping with it because it's hot, but it's a great way to keep the covers in place during your most restless nights.

The following few years were rocky as you continued to navigate your changing body, an influx of hormones, and academics.

Did it work, the candles and the avocados and the sheets pulled up tight?

I don't know. I may never know.

But as the wintry sky leaned into a lemon spring sun, your spirit eased the smallest bit.

YOU LOOKED up at me from your spot on the floor. Your face was tear-stained.

I walked slowly toward you as if you were a rare, delicate bird who would fly off into the clouds if I moved too quickly. When I reached you, you stood. I folded you in my mother-wings carefully, so carefully, not to wrap too tight.

Broken.

The word rose, unbidden, in my mind.

You laid your head on my shoulder, and we swayed together lightly, two leaves in a soft breeze. You wept, and I wept, too. I wept because of you and for you and with you.

"Take me. Home."

3

ACADEMIC JOURNEY

YOU WALK in the door at exactly 2:41, holding an envelope in your hands. Your cheeks are flushed pink. I assume it's from the chill outside because February isn't the kindest month in which to live in New Hampshire.

When I look closer, I realize it is neither wind nor temperature coloring your face. It's excitement.

~ ~

IT'S easy to assume our journey to this point started on a street in downtown Philadelphia, when we dropped your older brother off to a campus in the city. After a long car ride, we unloaded sheets, towels, books, and shampoo. You marveled at the small dorm room, your fingertips grazing the surface of the desk, the windowsill. You asked about having a roommate. It felt as though a seed had been planted.

College.

Yet, looking back, I wonder if it started earlier than that – in an empty classroom one green afternoon.

Out-of-district placement.

As autism's blizzard waged its springtime war within your 12-year-old spirit, this phrase began to pop up in my mind.

An out-of-district placement moves a student to a specialized school or program outside their local school district.

This is at the expense of either the district, the child's parents, or a combination of both. Out-of-district placements include specialized education schools, charter schools, and residential schools. Some schools are specialized for a particular disability (e.g., St. Joseph's School for the Blind), while others provide learning for students with various disabilities (e.g., ADHD, dyslexia, auditory processing disorder).

Students with more pervasive disabilities or significant mental health issues may require full-time residential placements.

Daddy and I went to a meeting in early June. The morning sun slanted in through the conference room windows. Familiar faces surrounded the table. One by one, each reported all the ways the year had gone wrong. Behaviors. Poor test grades. A field trip cut short.

"It seems we can no longer support Jack in public school."

This was no one's fault. Not the teachers, the paraprofessionals, or the recess monitors. Not yours. We all did the best we could – especially you. But at some point, autism made your corners sharper and more rigid, and it became harder and harder to wedge you into the round, smooth games at recess.

Still, it hurt. You couldn't make it in public school. This was the thought I returned to again and again.

Maybe I should have pushed harder. I should have sat at the counter and insisted you fill out the worksheets and study the outlines instead of packing it all away so soon. I should have communicated more with the team.

We all stood up, shuffling papers back into folders and pushing chairs under the table. I couldn't look at Daddy. I felt that one glance his way might dismantle all I was attempting to hold together.

I failed you.

My heartbreak was deeply intertwined with yours.

I always imagined all five of you crossing the same stage – five little ducklings in their caps and gowns. Never once did I imagine plucking one of them out of district.

For some reason, it was the bus that bothered me most.

In preschool, you took the small bus. Do you remember? There was an aide in the seat next to you; his name was Milton. Every morning, you trundled down the street and came back again at noon.

In first grade, you moved to the same elementary school as Joey. Once you understood this change, you made the case to share the same bus.

"I will ride. With Joey."

The school objected. During our meeting, the team was afraid it would be too loud. Without an aide, you might become deregulated and disruptive. On a bus with dozens of other kids, this could be dangerous. They recommended waiting, maybe switching you later in the year.

I knew with absolute certainty that they were right. It would be too loud, and there would be no Milton – and really, all hell could break loose at any moment during the five-mile drive to school and back again. But I also knew with absolute certainty that we had to give you a chance.

I remember I said only one thing – a single sentence: "We have to let him try."

On the first day of school, we walked down our long driveway to stand at the corner and wait. I reminded you to stay in your seat the entire ride. Still, I was worried we made the wrong decision. What if you started screaming or threw a fit? What if you couldn't handle the chatter and laughter around you?

The driver's name was Paul, and he was a kindly man with a gentle smile. He pulled up to the bus stop, waved a jovial wave, and shouted when I attempted to explain my concerns, "He'll be just fine!" and off you went on the big yellow bus. You never looked back.

Even this triumph, it seemed, would be taken away from you. Now, in your new school, you would be picked up in a white minivan. Your 6-year-old voice echoed in my mind.

"I ride the big bus. Like Joey. I go on the big bus."

Autism is heartbreak by one thousand papercuts. At times, it is the smallest, least predictable moments that give us pause.

Yet, at some point, we have to let go of our own dreams – our own agendas – in order to pursue a different path. This is where the work is.

~ ~

"JACK, buddy. Listen to me. You're going to a different school this year."

We'd just pulled into the garage after a trip to the grocery store. Sitting in the cool darkness, it was as if everything around us – Daddy's old work boots and the broom on the hook and the soccer ball in the corner – took a collective breath and waited.

It was August. The days were still long and hot, but there was a tinge of autumn in the air, especially at night. For weeks, there was an electric buzz in the house as the new school year approached. Talk of which pencils to buy, what time the bus would come, new teachers, and different classrooms.

You wanted blue pencils. You always wanted everything blue.

Sitting in the front seat, you turned to look at me. And you dissolved.

I held you across the console of our red minivan. Although I could feel the hate and rage and shame radiate off your body like the sun, for a moment, you let me hold you.

"Just let me be normal please let me go I will be good *please please please* I have to go I need a new start I will do it right I will be good like Joey I have to go like Joey."

I held you while you cried big, wet tears. I stroked your soft hair, and for a second, you laid your head in my lap. I rested my head on top of yours, and then, all at once, you lifted up, slamming into my chin. I bit my tongue. My own eyes welled.

"Why! For you. Are **CRYING**."

Oh, my Jack-a-boo, I thought.

I was crying for all the things you wouldn't have. A tuxedo for the prom. Hot lunch in a noisy cafeteria. The chance to stand at the bus stop with your three brothers and one sister on the first day of school.

YOUR FIRST DAY WAS ROUGH. You refused to get inside the minivan when it pulled up our driveway at 7:10 that morning. Reluctantly, you agreed to let me drive you. I clenched the steering wheel between my hands the entire ride there. Every few seconds, I glanced over at you. Your cheeks were tear-stained.

Once there, you wouldn't get out of the car. You stared straight ahead at the windshield.

After close to an hour, you agreed to step out onto the pavement. I met you around the other side, and we stood together, swaying in the parking lot.

I held both of your shoulders in my hands. I can still feel the way the fabric of your t-shirt slid between my fingers. I was so scared that if I let go, you would run off the sidewalk and into the parking lot and across the street and get hit by a car.

For nearly an hour, you wept. For an hour, we swayed together – deeply reminiscent of a springtime classroom. Every few minutes, you laid your head on my shoulder, and one single thought circled around and around in my mind like wispy smoke at a campfire.

Stay.

In that space of time, I thought of nothing else.

Stay with him.

At last, you turned and walked towards the door. Watching you walk inside with your shoulders slumped, I felt a combination of emotions swirled together – a watercolor muddied with deep blue sadness – but also buoyed with lemon-yellow hope.

THAT WAS SIX YEARS AGO.

In the last six years, you grew. You healed. You learned. We built you a cocoon, and inside of the darkness, you found light. All that was seemingly lost was replaced by better, gentler things.

Field trips to kayak down white-capped rivers, your mouth thrown open with laughter in the digital photo.

Worksheets done on beanbag chairs, testing administered in softly-lit rooms. Instead of the hustle and bustle of an over-crowded cafeteria, there is a small group around the table, and the occasional trip to the lunch truck parked outside.

Glasses with light blue frames give way to a darker navy. Shoe sizes go up and up until they finally settle at thirteen. Height, height, and more height – calling to mind the tallest sunflower against the sky – if sunflowers reach six-foot, five inches.

Finally, an unexpected graduation, crimson red cap upon your head, as you take deliberate steps in time to Pomp and Circumstance.

NOW, you sit next to me at the counter. Your brow furrows as you grip the pen and concentrate on signing your name.

For months, I have researched programs, college experiences, and vocational tracks. Using a website called www.thinkcollege.net, I scrolled through tabs and options. I set parameters for geographic distance, how much time students spend with neurotypical peers, and how much scaffolding is offered.

They all have chipper-sounding names. Strive. Reach. Sail. For reasons I can't quite explain, the names make me feel quietly unmoored. Will you be infantized forever?

I spend hours on the phone each afternoon, trying to hold paper descriptions against reality the way one might hold a candle in a window. The flame flickers every time I discover a new detail not revealed in the lively glow of online faces.

One admitted to locking up the food at night. Limited access to cabinets and the refrigerator. Using my best blue-point pen, I crossed it off right away.

Another insisted on a four-year degree. My pen hovered over paper, uncertain. In the end, I made an asterisk.

Last year, our mailbox was flooded with bumper stickers, pennants, and even a small teddy bear – sales propaganda sent from colleges hoping to win your brother Joey over to their campus.

Now, it sits mostly empty except for the everyday detritus of bills and catalogs.

Sail, Strive, and Excel, it seems, need no propaganda. They don't need marketing teams to fill their classrooms. As it is, there aren't enough spots for a burgeoning population of neurodiverse students looking for an opportunity beyond their front door.

Still, you check it every afternoon after school. You notice. I know you do. I notice, too.

In my most bitter moments, I file it away. I consider it one more way in which society rejects you. I hurt. I am angry.

On my softer days, I remind myself we are lucky to have something at all. Other people would long for our problems.

Yet, within each phone call and email is a sales pitch of my own. Yes, I tell them. You are medication compliant. You willingly take the pills that regulate your sleep, take the edge off your anxiety, and keep your depression at bay. You know how to order refills.

Yes, your hygiene is good. You shower every day. You shave carefully with an electric razor the way Daddy taught you. You can do laundry and prepare a meal. You have a bank account and a debit card for spending.

Carefully, I detail your vulnerabilities. The inability to read cues or create a meaningful connection. Trouble with social inferencing – understanding the different roles people play in life and interacting accordingly. A tendency to reject peers.

Instead of SAT scores, we submit proof of diagnosis, lists of medication, and the newest psychology report from your senior year.

In many ways, I am preparing another cocoon.

What choice do I have?

Come May, all of your services come to an end. There will be nowhere for you to go. Nothing for you to do. It will just be you and I coming up with activities and errands. Inside these walls, you will slowly turn into a man. I think it's more than either of us can bear.

In the end, we narrow it down to three.

One close to Boston, with a first-year transition program and then the opportunity to work toward a degree.

One in Connecticut, where you would live in a dorm and take classes with the support of a peer hired for this purpose. There are weekly meetings.

The third – and the one that I hope for the very most – is three hours away. A fully scaffolded residential space, with staff from 7:00 am until 11:00 pm. Academic teams. A life coach. A suite with a roommate and a kitchenette. Regular social outings and group activities.

The first two rejections come within days of each other. The language is similar, typed in black ink on white letterhead. I wonder if it's a generic form letter or personalized to you. To us.

"Unfortunately, your son is not the right fit at this time." I tossed them in the recycling bin.

Now, collectively, we hold our breath.

You see, Jack-a-boo, autism is a game of short strides. It is a million small steps and tiny decisions and pocket-size goals.

One day, you look up and realize all the work, all the hope, all the fear, all the worry is turning into something bigger than you imagined.

One day, you look up, and the world is glowing pink.

"Mom. This is a letter. It says I am accepted."

4

TO MY OLDEST, THE LETTER I NEVER WANTED TO WRITE

AT FIRST, we called you *Bean*.

Then, a variety of other nicknames: Beanie-boo, Buca, Boochie.

For the longest time, the world called you Joey, an informal iteration of the name on your birth certificate.

Now, at nineteen, you prefer Joseph.

My oldest son.

My firstborn child.

Daddy says he remembers the clock in the delivery room was white with black numbers. He checked it just as you made your appearance into the world – 12:34 on a Saturday morning in late March.

I remember your hair as they carried you away. It was damp and slick, but there was a lot of it. Dark, with the slightest wave.

I flopped back on the pillow, exhausted yet jubilant. I was a mother. After an early miscarriage, months of tearful trying, and the eternity of pregnancy, here you were. I was ready. I knew just what to do.

I was not ready. I did not know what to do.

Oh, sure! In the hospital, you were calm. You nestled into me and attempted to nurse. Visitors came and snuggled your soft limbs against their collarbone. Meals arrived regularly. Daddy changed all your diapers. Nurses took you away at night and brought you back at regular intervals.

That lasted, oh, twenty-four hours.

Twenty-four hours after I pushed a human out of my body, I was sitting in a car heading home. You were in the back seat, quiet for the most part. Daddy clenched his jaw and drove through streets that were previously unthreatening but now posed all kinds of hidden dangers to his tiny son. Potholes. Fast drivers. Traffic cones and yellow lights.

There is nothing like the first day at home with an infant. Time suspends within itself. Is it daytime? Or evening? We carried you inside and set you down on the rug. In your infant car seat, you looked minuscule – your skinny legs calling to mind a baby bird. We just stared at you.

I went upstairs to take a nap. When I woke up, you were both gone. I stumbled downstairs, wondering where a new father and his newborn son could possibly go. A few minutes later, you both came through the door. Daddy's face was lit and smiling. He had walked you from house to house, showing his firstborn off to all the neighbors. He was fiercely proud of you.

That night, you screamed for hours. The three of us slept in your tiny nursery – Daddy and I squashed on a twin mattress, you in what seemed like a cavernous crib.

You screamed, and we looked at each other with wild eyes. What did you need? How could a baby who was angelic in the hospital unleash such a sound? Daddy swaddled you and cradled your squirming body against his own, murmuring a *shh-shh-shh* sound over and over while I wondered what on earth I'd done.

I tell this not to elicit feelings of guilt – but to let you know one day, you may experience your own feelings of regret-tinged love. It's normal, especially with a newborn.

After that night, by most counts, you were an easy baby. You were easily soothed. You smiled and cooed.

At the same time, I underestimated the day-to-day grind of it all. The pacifiers, the burping clothes, the spit-up trailing down my back. No one quite prepares a new mother for the minutiae that accompanies taking care of a tiny human – how endlessly needy an infant can seem.

I remember your first word so clearly. The three of us were standing in the kitchen. Daddy held you facing outward while I teased out the syllables you announced earlier that afternoon.

"Cook-IE."

His face lit up, and he laughed out loud. You repeated again and again, looking back at him with a grin on your face.

Nineteen.

In the very beginning, you called me *Mama*. You toddled around the living room shakily with your arms in the air and called for me.

Mama Mama Mama.

At some point, you started to call me *Mommy.*

Mommy, where are you?

Mommy, I want a banana.

Mommy, my tummy hurts.

The change was so gradual I hardly noticed. Eventually, it became *Mom.*

Mom, I failed the math test.

Mom, I think she likes me.

Mom, can I borrow the car?

When you were four, all you wanted to wear was a shirt with the numbers zero and seven on it. It was white with green sleeves. You loved it so much I bought a second one just like it, in case the first wasn't clean. In your tiny voice, you asked again and again, "Oh seven? My oh seven shirt?"

Today, you are nineteen.

Nineteen is college, Crossfit, classes in finance.

It is a girlfriend and a city apartment.

It is weekly calls home and trips for spring break and, overall, a life of your own.

My son.

In some ways, this is a letter I never wanted to write.

I am counting on you.

Of course I am. How could it be any other way?

It isn't fair.

I know.

I used to think life was fair.

Then autism came on the scene in the shape of a 9-pound, 3-ounce baby boy named Jack. Your brother. And my mind was forever changed.

It isn't fair that once your father and I are no longer here, the responsibility will fall to you.

I'll never know what that is like for you.

I'll never know what any of it was like for you.

You are an Autism Brother. And this is no small thing.

Autism has been the tympani of your background since you were thirteen months old. It is the only life you've ever known – a lifetime of people staring at us in airports, movies cut short, and restaurant outings that ended in disaster.

It's always been you.

It was you he toddled after on chubby legs, an everlasting circle of brother-following-brother.

It was you he watched kick, throw, run. And then he announced his first word as though he'd been storing it up all along.

Ball.

It was you who taught him how to tie his sneakers, looping one through the other and pulling them tight.

It was you he watched climb the steps of the big yellow bus. He insisted he could, too.

He chases you. He always has.

It's not fair. It's not fair that your peers think of only their own lives, their own happiness, their own paths, while you must think of him.

The truth is: fair left the building a long time ago.

Oftentimes, caring for a complicated child can feel like a deep black hole in which there are no answers. Now, perhaps more than ever, I worry about what will happen when *I die*.

Daddy and I have made arrangements. He'll be taken care of financially. He'll likely live in a supported environment. You won't have to worry about the day-to-day stuff.

He won't rely on you. But he will need you. Still, I worry.

Please, don't let him spend Christmas alone.

Call him. Check on him. Make sure he's okay.

Buy his favorite cookies when he comes to visit.

Sit with him. Listen to him talk.

In other words, do all the things you already do.

Do you remember the time you ran away?

I think you were in the fourth grade. We'd argued about homework. As you stuffed your folders back into your backpack, I turned to the stove and started dinner. When it was time to eat, we called and called for you, but you didn't answer.

We ran outside to look for footprints in the dusting of snow that coated the driveway throughout the early evening, but it was nothing more than a velvet blanket in darkness.

Back inside the house, we called your name. My heartbeat rang inside my ears. We looked in closets and the basement.

Then, from underneath your bed, a small shadow. You emerged, your face tear-stained.

It was that night when I resolved to make my parenting less about worksheets and flashcards and more about cookies at the kitchen counter.

Now, childhood is coming to a close for you.

One day, how will you look back on this time? What will you remember?

I hope you remember the way he set the table, awaiting your return from wherever the afternoon had taken you.

I hope you remember how your father dragged us from dealership to dealership, researching cars with every safety feature available, imagining his special son may one day sit behind the wheel.

I hope you remember all the times I made room for you, even when autism took up a lot of space.

We are an autism family.

We are full of small slights and petty resentments and belly laughs and birthday cake on white plates.

We root for the underdog.

We take care of our own.

Autism is our house.

We are flawlessly imperfect, but we are honest.

We love him.

We know him.

Autism is a listener's language. It speaks to those who hear — those who seek to understand.

Still, we struggle for fluency. We become impatient, we talk too fast, we forget to listen.

We are learning.

Yet you were always his voice, even when the rest of us couldn't find the words.

This house has windows and doors and lots of light. It has a strong foundation and a table with lots of seats.

We built it for him.

You grant him freedom beyond autism's golden cage.

You see, you are not only his brother. You are everyone's brother. You are one of many who live alongside autism — who hear the iPads bounce, watch the raging tantrums, and feel the awkward stares as strangers work to make sense of our lives.

Through a complicated twist of genetic fate, he became a statistic, while you became who you are.

Because of autism, our family is one plot on a scatter chart of many. We are a percentage.

For the most part, your life will carry on as expected. It might follow the college-job-marriage-child trajectory, while in some ways, he will stand still. Like a rare bird inside a gilded cage, he will remain confined by the constraints autism has imposed upon him.

Please, when I'm gone.

Take care of him.

I know.

It isn't fair.

But I have to ask it of you.

Take care of him. Please.

He loved you first.

Mostly, what I want to say is: please remember. Remember that in the moments I yelled or criticized or frowned, I loved you still.

Still, I loved you.

I love you.

I want to remind you that on your worst of days , when you feel overwhelmed and lost and lonely. When the rain won't stop, and the sun won't shine – remember our walks on the beach and the seashells in your hand.

Remember the way we curled up on the deep red couch as the thunder rolled and the lightning flashed. The secret stories we told with a warm dog nestled beside us.

Remember that even when I was busy folding, shopping, cooking, driving, managing meltdowns, or reading IEP reports, I *never* lost sight of you. You never left my mind.

My oldest boy, my first son, my child called Joseph.

Time is spinning faster and faster – an hourglass full of slippery sand.

Now that you live in the city of love and eagles, I find it is the smallest things I miss the most. Giant shoes outside the door. Your quick goodbye and easy laugh. The sound of the car up the long driveway.

I know there are hard days ahead of you.

Days when you will make a wrong turn.

A mistake.

A bad decision.

You will lose your judgment and find it again.

Maybe you won't get the job or the promotion or the house you wanted.

Life can be full of an uncountable messiness. Miscarriages, divorce, traffic tickets.

Colicky babies, loud arguments, tax bills.

In the hardest moments, I can only tell you three things.

Be honest.

Be brave.

Be yourself.

For now, I will write for you all the words I did not say – the things that are lodged within my heart.

Make your bed in the morning. It's a good way to start the day.

Sing out loud to your favorite song, even if you don't know all the words.

Respect deadlines.

Don't be afraid to say no.

Eat when you're hungry.

Stop when you are full.

Dream big, delicious dreams for yourself. Then, figure out exactly how to make them come true.

Think critically about the world around you.

Hold the door for others.

Be curious.

Ask questions.

And listen for the answer.

Read.

Pray.

Vote.

Practice yoga.

And no matter what, on dark, rainy mornings and bright, sunny afternoons, days when you are homesick and sad, or happy and triumphant.

Days when the mistakes feel so big, and you are hopeless and alone.

Please, remember.

Mama loves you.

5

FRIENDSHIP

I GUESS you could say coincidence brought us together. We just happened to pick the right seats.

In a dusty classroom, we sat around a large table, comparing notes about finance. Or was it statistics? Time has eroded that detail, yet I vividly remember you wearing a blue sweater. I can still see the sun setting through the windows – golden bars of light spreading across the carpet. We introduced ourselves.

"Hi, I'm Melissa."

"I'm Carrie."

It was the fall of 1995. We were earnest students finishing up a Master's degree at Rockefeller College in downtown Albany, New York.

From that point on, we were study buddies, confidantes, and friends. We spent weekend afternoons shopping at the mall – trying on shoes, sweaters, and clearance-rack jackets. We talked about everything from boyfriends to books.

Once we graduated, our lives were set to follow a similar path: Degree, jobs, wedding, kids.

On a warm summer Saturday, I married my college sweetheart. Two weeks later, as the green leaves began to tinge with orange, you married yours. Dressed in white, we bravely stood on our mutual dance floors and clapped our hands to the beat.

Fast forward, oh, maybe five years from the dancing and the white. We'd started our families – four little boys between us. You were one of the first people I called.

"The doctor said he has autism."

We'd talked about it before, of course. We compared notes the way all mothers do. How many hours a baby should sleep, when our older sons started walking, if I should be concerned that Jack couldn't manage solid food at eight months.

During our phone call, you listened. You let me talk. I just had to get the words out without someone interrupting to soothe me or to tell me it was going to be okay.

I could hear your own toddler in the background asking for juice.

Jack never asked me for juice.

He never asked me for anything.

He was what they call *self-directed*. If he felt like having juice, he just ambled on over to the refrigerator and attempted to get it himself by scaling the shelves. This usually ended in a few broken eggs if I didn't get to him in time.

The truth is, I didn't even know what I needed. I was still turning this diagnosis over like a copper penny in the palm of my hand. I did know I was at the beginning of something, even if I didn't understand what.

Autism Spectrum Disorder.

Cradling the phone between my ear and my shoulder, I steered Jack toward the television. I put a Baby Einstein DVD in and pushed play. I could sense he was getting antsy, and I was on borrowed time. I glanced over at 3-year-old Joey, sitting at the table eating applesauce while the baby, 6-month-old Charlie, napped upstairs.

I thought about my husband, Joe, at work filling cavities and chatting with patients, the black-and-white diagnosis swirling in his mind while he went about his day.

I felt hungry, yet nauseous.

"I don't know yet. I'll call you tomorrow, okay?"

And I did. When you answered, I blurted out the news like my tongue was on fire – news that explained the simultaneous hunger pangs and nausea.

"I'm pregnant."

I called you the following day, and the next. And when life got in the way and phone calls became too challenging with toddler demands, school pick-ups, and eventually, sports, we turned to daily emails. Monday through Friday every single week.

When people first hear of Jack's diagnosis, they often *"you should"* me.

You should do more research.

You should find another doctor.

You should take gluten out of his diet.

On the heels of *"you should"* is *"at least."*

At least he is talking.

At least you have other kids.

At least you have the money for therapies.

You never said either.

You let me complain about the ordinary grind that can be life alongside a young child with autism – the need for routine and structure. The ongoing process of finding the right program and school setting. The long-term fear of my own mortality nagging at me from beneath my ribcage.

You listened to it all without judgment. When I said I was tired, you never jumped in with your own story of fatigue. You never sought to normalize my challenges by wearing them as your own.

Through the years, I know you were worried about sharing all the great things your kids did with me – all the milestones and achievements. You worried it might hurt me to watch your children leap forward while this boy of mine stood still.

Were there moments I was jealous? Sure. Yes. But I was always happy for you and, by extension, proud of your kids.

Autism's papercuts can sting when we least expect it. But for the most part, they are quick. Fleeting. We breathe through the hurt and get back to our day.

If life alongside autism has taught me anything, it's that I can celebrate and hurt at the exact same time. Both things can be true.

You made your home a safe landing for our family. So often, I felt trapped by the outside world, as though it was hemming us in from the edges. There were so few places we could go – so few people who understood what it was like to invite a family over whose toddler might start the car or need all the lights turned down low.

In the beginning, simple errands were harder and harder. One day, he went berserk in the grocery store. He smashed an entire jar of spaghetti sauce on the floor. At two years old, his strength was admirable. He fiercely committed to his rage – it emanated from deep inside my little boy like red-hot lava from a volcano.

You kept his favorite snacks in the cabinet. Goldfish crackers and pretzel rods. You made sure your kids knew that Jack was coming, and if there was something they didn't want dismantled or broken, it was best to put it away. I always appreciated the boundaries. It was a way we could make sure he was successful. It helped me relax that much more.

You never minded when he opened your refrigerator and took out the ketchup, the mustard, the pickles, making a tall tower of jars on the kitchen floor. You showed him the playlists you created with him in mind. Together, you played music that rang through the kitchen.

He loved to go through your DVDs, sorting them into an order only he understood. One afternoon, you looked over at him, surrounded by discs and plastic covers, and you smiled. Your ease meant everything. It helped me find my own.

Most of the time, once we arrived, I'd flop on your couch in my favorite yoga pants and just breathe. You kept your expectations low. You understood that simply getting out of the house with kids and autism may have taken every ounce of energy I had.

Autism was a freely spoken word at your table. Your kids knew it. Your husband embraced it. You never kept my son a secret. Inside your home, a small army of advocates was born.

You loved him.

You love him still.

You love his anxiety, his quirkiness, his lack of filter.

Dear friend, on my darkest marital days, you reminded me that I do indeed love this man. Sure, you nodded your head and agreed he was an idiot. You rolled your eyes when I described managing infants and toddlers while he strolled through the door ten minutes late. You shrugged your shoulders and sighed in disgust when I explained how he dumps all the stuff out of his pockets onto the kitchen counter.

Then you gently mentioned all the tender ways he shows up for me. Coffee in the morning. A hug before dinner. You reminded me of our history together – how we met on a sunlit campus, and the first thing he did was offer to carry my books.

On the days I sank to a whisper, you were my voice. At half-time, you told the other parents in the bleachers why I had to leave the game early. During storytime, you gathered the rest of my kids into your circle as I paced the hallway outside with a thrashing boy.

When puberty struck our house like a wild storm, you never claimed to have the answers. You didn't try to solve the puzzle of medication, self-harm, and rage that was my son. And when my urge to catastrophize and think of every worst-case scenario possible, you quietly suggested other outcomes.

We are about as opposite as two women can be. I am impulsive and somewhat emotional to your calmness and your practicality. You take forever to order from the menu or to choose a pair of jeans; I buy it first and think later.

We mother differently. You are warm and nurturing. You hold your children close while I long to let mine loose.

Some might say we balance each other out – the proverbial yin to the yang. However you package it, we offer a different perspective every time. A fresh look at the ordinary aspects of life. To me, this is the invaluable, intangible aspect of a lasting friendship.

Dear friend, forgive me for all the times I withdrew – when I didn't ask you enough about your life. When I faded into the background, disappeared from book club meetings, or declined invitations. You see, there were moments on this journey when I simply needed to cocoon for a bit. I needed to turn inward and nurse my private musings.

From the very beginning, you rooted for me as I started this uphill climb. You rooted for me even on days when I couldn't root for myself.

You know everything about me.

My familial baggage, my insecurities, my weakness for sugar cookies, and a great pair of boots.

My mistakes, my petty jealousy, my bitterness, my anger, my darkness.

Still, you loved me.

You love me still.

Always, you believed. You believed in the copper penny, the future, the boy himself.

I was talking to a young woman at a cocktail party recently. She had an earnestness about her that reminded me of our younger selves. She told me her nephew had just been diagnosed with autism. She wondered how to help her sister as she began her own walk down this rocky path.

I told her, "Do what my friend did."

Listen without interruption.

Be gentle.

Make space in your home.

Root from the sidelines.

Buy snacks.

And if she announces an unexpected pregnancy the day after a diagnosis, tell her one thing and one thing only.

"That is so exciting."

It's been nearly three decades since that golden blue autumn evening in New York.

For thirty years, I have sat at my computer every morning and, fingers poised over the keyboard, written to you. These fifteen minutes were my therapy, my meditation, my outlet, my saving grace. They helped me order my thoughts and untangle my emotions. In many ways, they helped shape me into a writer. Because of you, I learned how to tell our story.

I don't know what we were studying back in that dusty classroom, it's true. But I do know one thing.

I couldn't have done it without you.

6

CONSTRUCTION ZONES

"CAN I go back to the car and get my water?"

I REMEMBER it was warm that day, warmer than usual for October. The sun was brilliant overhead.

I was hungry, *starving*, actually. We'd left in a hurry right after I went running. The drive took over an hour – even longer to find parking in a nearby garage. We made it to the bridge with just a few minutes to spare.

The morning had already been fraught with tension. Daddy was out of town, and at first, I told Rose I couldn't make her crew meet in Boston because I promised you we'd go shopping for new clothes.

She got a little, uh, huffy. Not overtly so, because teenage girls are rarely overt in their disdain, but I could tell she was upset.

I rethought our plans. We could head into Boston, watch her row, and maybe get some lunch. We had the whole weekend to shop. Then it was *your* turn to get huffy. In our family of seven, no one is ever happy at the same time.

M.O.M. – Manager of Moods. This was perhaps the most unexpected aspect of motherhood for me. No one prepared me for how much – or how hard – I would work to make everyone happy. How my maternal red flags would constantly rise in response to the energy of my husband and my kids.

I turned to you on the bridge. You were standing to my right. Nearly as tall as me, you slouched over as though you'd just come off a 12-hour graveyard shift, and now you had to figure out how to pay the electric bill. I narrowed my eyes.

"Sure, go. I'm sick of listening to you complain."

"Mom, are you sure?" Charlie shifted on my left. "He doesn't have a phone."

"He'll be fine," I assured him. "Rose's boat will be here any second now. We'll watch her and then follow him back to the garage. It will only be a few minutes."

I looked over my shoulder and saw you walk away, my youngest son, a silhouette beneath the dazzling autumn sky, all skinny arms and gangly legs. I looked back down at the water. As expected, the boats glided beneath us – so many silent torpedoes cutting through coolness. I caught a glimpse of Rose's curly hair under her visor.

～ ～

THE BANTER in our family has always been that you were unexpected, a mistake, even. It's a timeworn story told again and again – how I walked downstairs and showed Daddy the positive pregnancy test. Speechless, he covered his eyes.

Thirteen years ago, you made your arrival. Except you didn't just arrive into the world. You roared. All ten pounds, four ounces, twenty-one inches of you. Your labor was so fast that there wasn't time for any pain medication. It could be said there were two of us roaring.

CHARLIE and I turned from the water. We walked the length of the bridge and up the path leading to the parking garage. We walked with purpose. Not hurried, but not slow. We reached the car – a new Toyota Highlander we'd bought a month earlier, after the minivan, affectionately nicknamed *The Red Hot Chili Pepper*, reached almost 200,000 miles.

You weren't there.

Henry. Hen-Ben. Hendrixon. Your nicknames floated through my consciousness like so many butterflies.

It is shocking how quickly impatience turns to panic. You wouldn't think the human heart could switch gears so fast.

At the exact same time, the human brain can cover a lot of ground. Perhaps even more than a 13-year-old afoot in a city littered with construction sites and parking garages.

Images fought for space in my mind.

Chubby infant, mischievous toddler, gangly 8th grader.

My son.

Stuffing peas up your nose during dinner.

Piecing Legos together at the kitchen table.

Blinking back tears as the doctor wrapped a cast around your broken leg.

You always hated to be last. When you were in kindergarten, you raced to get on the bus first so often, I worried you'd get run over in the street. If we were late to anywhere – a barbecue, a birthday party – you became agitated.

We likened you to a pot on the stove. We urged you to simmer rather than boil when you became elevated and loud. When you struggled to pay attention, we told you to think of your brain as a flashlight. We used it as a tactic for focus, reminding you to shine your light when you needed to look for your shoes, your homework folder, and your gloves in winter.

There is a phenomenon in our house we call *leapfrogging* – when a younger sibling passes by Jack in skill or maturity. It is always painful for both. Now, at thirteen to his eighteen, you've officially leapt past him. This has brought a lot of conflict between the two of you. From the sidelines, I watch. I ache for each of you: older brother longing for status, younger brother uncertain of his new role.

Now, on the streets of Boston, you could be anywhere.

Where are you?

Where did you go?

Unless you've been tasked with locating a lost puppy or a misplaced child, it's hard to comprehend the concept of *anywhere*. Anywhere is every coffee shop, every vehicle, every park, every highway. It is massive. It is immense. The world expands.

I headed back to the bridge while 16-year-old Charlie stayed behind, checking the levels of the garage. As reluctant as I was to leave another child, I knew it was practical. He had a phone. We could stay in contact.

I scanned a construction site where huge pieces of equipment sat dormant. I called your name.

Henry.

Panic clutched my throat. My heart vibrated. Maybe you forgot we had a new car. Maybe you looked for the minivan. Maybe you went to the wrong floor of the parking garage.

Or maybe . . . worse. Maybe a lifetime of searching for a child I let go of too easily.

At some point, do I start screaming? When do I call the police and declare it an emergency? When do I set in motion the very thing I've always feared the most?

Losing a child.

I imagine the call to Daddy, the moment of silence while he absorbs the news that I couldn't find you. Plans would be made. He would fly home.

The picture haunts me. The one I took ten minutes before you walked off the bridge – when I posed you and Charlie together. It's the kind of picture people show to the police so they know what the missing person is wearing that day. It feels ominous, like foreshadowing.

Why did I say yes? Why did I let you go?

You complained you were thirsty.

You wanted your water bottle.

You were unhappy in the way a 13-year-old is often unhappy.

I was irritated in the way a mother of a 13-year-old is often irritated.

I told you to go.

I told you to go, and then I couldn't find you.

Don't mind me, my son, as I stretch my fingers to the hot flame of regret.

It's been weeks now. Some mornings, I wake at 4:00 am, heart pounding, mind racing.

Daddy sighs in his sleep next to me. In the early morning light, I revisit the water, the bridge, the sun.

I leave space for my ineptitude, my mistake, and my utter lapse in judgment.

As I heal ever so slightly, I remember: the best choices in life are made when we're resourced, rested, fed, connected.

Now, a new tenderness for you blossoms within me. At night, on the couch, I notice glints of red in your otherwise dark hair. I toast you late-night bagels and spread cream cheese. I bend my head close and hear your gentle laugh.

Just like that, panic becomes patience. This is the very gift bestowed upon me.

Tender mercies, I believe these are called. A new beginning.

This is motherhood. No one departs unshaken. Again and again, we are reborn.

I long for rules. I wish for black and white. In the end, I'm left with handfuls of color.

Why did I let you go?

Slowly, I make friends with the monster under my bed. Together, we sit in the early light, and I whisper, he's here, this boy is here, he is down the hall under a Star Wars blanket, and he is *A-Okay*.

Mostly, I whisper a collection of words that remind me all is not gone. All is not lost.

On my knees beneath a starling sky, a second chance.

"Mom! I found him. I found Henry."

7

UNTETHERING

I READ SOMEWHERE that it's easy to trap bees in a jar. This is because they don't look up to the sky; they focus on the bottom – the proverbial floor beneath their wings.

Jack-a-boo, ever since you were born, I've joked that the umbilical cord between us never really severed. We orbit one another like two planets in a solar system. I don't know how else to describe it.

In fact, it was almost as though the space between us grew smaller as you got older. You are never far from me in the house. If you aren't in the same room as me, you call for me, checking where I am.

In many ways, I am your companion. You accompany me everywhere – the grocery store, the bank, out for lunch. A doctor once pointed out that you use me to regulate your own nervous system – my mood and regulation calibrate yours.

I find this an exhausting aspect of life alongside autism. The ability to perpetually stay calm and unruffled has never been my strong suit.

Over the years, I've adopted a few strategies that help me keep my voice even when all I want to do is scream.

A long-standing yoga practice, deep breaths in through the nose and out through the mouth are always good.

Keeping one hand spread over my clavicle – known to be the most relaxed position a person can have – helps bring my heart rate down.

I've walked out of the room before . . . when I wasn't confident I could hold it together while you looped and spiraled about everything from a perceived slight in school to an unanticipated change in the schedule.

Oddly enough, the tool that helps me the most is perhaps the simplest: a glass of water. When I feel like I might lose my ever-loving mind, I pour myself some water. I force myself to hold it between my hands and feel the chill of the glass. I look at the surface and notice the smooth stillness. I take tiny sips.

One time, when you were particularly elevated because we couldn't find the right measuring cup for baking brownies, I sat on the floor. I didn't say a single word. I simply walked over to the table and lowered myself onto the rug.

From the counter to the cabinet, you paced and muttered furiously, swearing under your breath.

"But WHERE IS IT. I NEED the small measuring cup. For the WATER and the OIL."

Your voice rose and fell in frustration. I didn't attempt to soothe you or suggest you choose better language. I sat still and looked at my hands in my lap. I willed myself to keep them folded. I reminded myself that sometimes, we all need a little interruption. The floor. The rug. Deep breaths. They provided just that.

Eventually, after what seemed like an eternity full of profanity, you joined me. Like a toy whose battery had run out, you slumped down and pressed your fingertips to your eyes to staunch the tears. Together, we sat until we were both ready to search for that measuring cup again.

You are nearly eighteen now. Still, we remain explicably bound. I'm so used to it that I hardly notice anymore.

Whenever I leave the house, I return to find you standing there, waiting, when I pull into the garage. You ask where I've been, what I did, why I was gone so long. And every afternoon, at exactly 2:37, your voice rings out into the kitchen.

"For Mom! I am home."

In many ways, we are like the bees. We scrutinize the jar. We examine the walls and the floor. We stare at one another instead of shifting our gaze toward the horizon.

Autism has connected us together in the complicated ways. For eighteen years, we were a "we."

I spoke when you couldn't find the words.

I fought for you. I sat in stuffy conference rooms and made a case for inclusion and speech. I asked questions on your behalf.

Every time we entered a building, I scanned for an exit in case we needed to leave quickly or early.

I watched people stare; their expressions changed when they noticed you jump in place or twitch your fingers.

And even as you grew taller than me, you still held my hand when we crossed the parking lot.

When you became a teenager, I substituted my frontal lobe for yours – counseling you on everything from schoolwork to how the caffeine in soda will keep you awake at night to the best way to change the sheets on your bed. It was too hard to let you stumble and learn on your own.

Even something as simple as ordering in a restaurant kept me on the edge of my seat, scanning your face and then the server's face for any misundestanding or confusion.

Essentially, I interpreted the world-to-boy and the boy-to-world. I interfaced between you both until I was blue in the face.

"Hi, yes, this is my son Jack. He has autism."

"Jack, go ahead now, order your cheeseburger."

"Oh, yes, he loves ketchup, thank you!"

"Jack, tell her, yes, you'd like ketchup with it. Make sure to say please!"

In a few months' time, you will move to a college program.

I don't know what I'll do with myself. All the everyday tasks and responsibilities will vanish into thin air.

Appointments.

Medication.

Schedule.

I never quite grasped how deeply my nervous system was intertwined with yours – how I rode the autism emotional rollercoaster every single day – until I considered that the ride may one day sit still.

In many ways, I built my life around you. I didn't choose this. It is simply motherhood with a diagnosed child.

Weekends were especially hard. Beginning Friday afternoons at 3:00 until the bus came Monday morning, I had to fill your hours, your afternoons, your early evenings.

Technology doesn't exactly help this, as you rely on your phone for endless communication with me. Texts to share every thought you have. Questions about my mood, our day, the house, the dog. Grocery lists, requests for another song from iTunes, offhand messages about the weather.

It's so easy to give in – to answer every message and try to solve your problems and help you stay calm. It is a familiar pattern. But it won't do you any favors.

It is time to begin the long, slow process of untethering from you – of at last breaking the seemingly permanent cord between us.

We were tempted to keep you here – in this town, this life, this house. Like a bird in a gilded cage, we longed to protect you.

Yet we didn't.

We opened the door and encouraged you to stretch your wings across the sky.

I want you to fly.

Yet, I am conflicted about the separation.

After all, nothing cuts quite as deep as autism's two-sided sword.

This is the stuff no one talks about. No one talks about the inevitable codependency that develops when you raise a son who the world struggles to understand. No one talks about the heartache of pulling back from your own vulnerable child.

Now, I need to do the very hard work of untangling my own needs from your future. As the winter branches sway inside an icy wind, I sit at my desk and wonder how to accomplish this.

I lean back in my chair.

With my hands – index fingers reaching wide – I touch my thumbs together to form a W.

We.

Slowly, I separate the thumbs and tuck them beneath my palms, index fingers stretched skyward.

I.

This is the invisible road we must travel – nothing more than fingertips spreading from one letter of the alphabet to another.

We to I.

I decide – as is often the case with autism and progress – to start with baby steps.

I begin putting the phone aside when I hear the text alert. I answer maybe every third message. I give you an outline of when I'll be available throughout the day.

"But what," you ask, "if I need you more?"

"You've got this," I assure you.

Gently, my own heart heavy, I suggest you wait inside the house when I pull up the driveway. I point out how your brothers and sister don't rush to the door when they hear the car. They greet me once I walk into the kitchen.

You started managing your own medication around eleven – reminding me for refills and shaking the small pills into your hand every evening. Now, I think you're ready to take this level of independence even further.

Using my laptop at the kitchen counter, I introduce you to the online portal through the doctor's office. I take you through each step, from logging in with your password to sending the doctor a message when it's time to order a new prescription.

Sitting next to you in a restaurant, I busy myself with my own menu while you look at yours. The server stands at our table with pen poised over pad. I bite my tongue and resist the urge to edit your choice.

"For yes. I would like the cheeseburger. No pickle, no onion, no tomato, no lettuce."

"Sure thing! How would you like it cooked?"

"On a stove," you answer. And after a second of hesitation, "Please."

I watch you order yet another soda, and force myself not to comment on the correlation between caffeine and sleeplessness. These are your dots to connect now.

Instead of interpreting boy-to-world, it is your turn to offer your own explanation.

Slowly, I slide from interpreter to mother – meddler to bystander.

For the most part, it seems to be working. I feel a loosening of sorts. You call for me less. And one day, side-by-side at the counter of a diner, a smooth conversation without interruption.

"For yes. I would like a cheeseburger for my lunch today."

{ heartbeat }

"Please."

This is good, I tell myself. We are moving in the right direction, even if my heart is squeezing just the tiniest bit.

Yesterday, as the ice on the driveway melted to slush, I pulled into the garage. For the first time, you weren't standing at the door. I turned the car off, put my head on the steering wheel, and cried.

What am I doing?

See, buddy, in this autism life, there is no manual. There are no instructions for how to untie yourself from a tender child, one who needed you for so long that you forgot what life was like before he disrupted your world in an exquisitely magical way.

I don't want to let go.

At the same time, I don't want you to wait for me another moment.

I don't want you to watch the world through glass. I wanted you to reach out and know your own sky.

My son.

I will always be here for you. Even as the texts go quiet and the advice lessens. It is simply time for me to root from the sidelines. I have to disentangle myself from your story, even as I long to stay a main character. It is the only way to help you build a life full of richness and color.

From we to I.

We to I.

We.

I.

For so long, you were a bee.

Now, you are the shimmering wave that meets the shore. You are the colorful cloud overhead. You are possibility wrapped up in a new beginning.

You are a tender heart wrapped in mystery.

"I always came to do the door. To see if you needed me to bring groceries in."

Growth is disruptive.

Building a family is messy.

It was in the dishwasher the whole time, remember? The measuring cup. Charlie used it for his protein shake.

8

WINTER'S STARS

SLEEP NOW, sweet baby.

Curl against me and close your eyes. Although the past few hours were easy by childbirth's standards, we are both tired.

My third boy, my middle son, my dark-haired infant.

Charles Patrick Cariello.

This is the name we landed on in the hospital as you leisurely made your way into the world. Like your brothers before you, there will be various renditions of your moniker: Char-Char, Charlums, Charlie-bear.

I have no idea where we came up with Patrick. Over the next few years, I'll change this bit of history and insert my maiden name instead, perhaps wishing I weaved a bit of my own heritage into our family. *Charles Watterson Cariello*, I'll call from the bottom of the stairs, through the bathroom door, or out into the dusky night as you bounce a basketball.

Right now, it is just you and me in this room with the lights down low and the softly humming machines. The doctor who supervised your arrival is long gone. Daddy went home to relieve the sitter and make dinner for your brothers.

We are alone, and it feels like we are the only two people in the universe. I straighten the light blue cap on your head and re-wrap your striped blanket. I glance out the window as the November sun fades weakly in the sky. I hear nurses bustling in the hallway. I wonder what color your eyes will be.

Let me hold you close, here and now. In the next day or so, we'll head home – all cumbersome car seat and diaper bag – and within a week, everyone in the house except us will come down with a vicious stomach bug. This moment will be lost in the shuffle of feverish toddlers and disinfectant. In other words, ordinary life.

If we concentrate hard enough, little one, we can squint into the future and see all the different versions you become.

A young boy in dinosaur pajamas, earnestly coloring Easter eggs at the table.

The first day of preschool, bright blue backpack and wide grin.

Small, outstretched palms, shaking from a nightmare about Big Foot coming into your room.

A fourth grader, standing alongside a rotating vacuum cleaner at the science fair – noticeably taller, the baby fat melted from limbs and face.

A cannonball on the first day of summer, splashing into the glittering pool.

The new driver – walking confidently from the parking lot to announce passing the test on the first try.

Buffalo Bills fan, cheering from the couch with your father on Sunday afternoons.

Boy, more akin to a kite, chasing the wind as I wave from the ground and hold tightly to the strings.

Varsity baseball player, delivering pitch after pitch on the mound. In the waning light, the throws vary – sliders, curve-balls, and changeups. But the concentrated brow and determination never waver.

When the coach is stern and the straggly crowd heckles from the bleachers, I will return to this day. I will think of the soft curve of your newborn face and how you sighed as you dozed in my arms.

Sweet baby of mine, let me hold you close.

Let me whisper all the secrets I know in your ear. Let me tell you everything.

The truth is you were born straight into autism's chaos. Even as I trace your tiny nose and rosebud lips in this hospital room, I worry about what might unfold at home. Will Jack eat what Daddy made? Will he throw food on the floor and race around the table? Will he sleep tonight?

I force myself back to you instead. I know how precious our time is here together. I know a third child in as many years will make life feel hamster-wheel busy.

In many ways, a family is a stage where we each choose our roles. In our house, autism provides the music to which we dance: violent drums one day, melancholy flutes the next.

You will know his heart. I don't know how else to describe it.

You will draw him out into your jokes, your dance parties, and your games on the front lawn.

As your mother, I have many memories. The first loose tooth, t-ball on Saturday mornings, the last time you needed training wheels. A broken arm, trips to the playground, tall sandcastles at the beach.

But this room has the strongest foothold in my mind's eye. It is where I return again and again.

Stay afloat.

One day, as the leaves glow with bursts of orange and gold, I'll stand in the kitchen and whisper these words to you. My head meets your shoulder. You eclipsed me in height long ago.

To the casual observer, you are the kid who has it all. A quick smile, lots of friends, good grades. Yet the time will come when your heart breaks into pieces like only a teenage heart can break.

Stay afloat.

Night after night, this is what we tell you, our dark-haired son. When you wake us at dawn, panicked and frantic. When you can't eat, sleep, study, or laugh. When you have trouble simply getting out of bed each morning.

Where did he go?

This is the question I will ask myself as the ground becomes a carpet of autumn confetti.

Where did my sunny, cheerful son disappear to?

The one who sat beside me in the car, laughing until his cheeks flushed pink?

Who stepped off the rubber mound after a chilly game and headed straight to Target to buy a birthday present for his diagnosed brother?

It's as though your battery ran out – this boy of endless jokes and impeccable imitations. You were the easy one, the child I could take my eyes off from time to time. Yet I took my gaze off you for a moment too long, and you sank.

Silently, I worried that I relied on you to be easy for too long. I relied on your storytelling, breeziness, and endless capacity for fun to liven up the dinner table.

You turned to holiday decorations. Alone in the cold, you hung hundreds of Christmas lights, hoping to forget a girl. Night after night, you stood atop a ladder and looped the strands through trees and over eaves.

There is no such thing as an easy child. That's the problem. There is a child who figures out how to fly under the radar – how to reduce his own needs in the face of autism's storms. A child who stands alone, shivering in the hallway, afraid something bigger than all of us might swallow him whole.

A heart-shaped rock from the ball field. This will be my most precious gift, offered in an offhand way after I missed a game. Gently, I will place it on the bookshelf in my bedroom.

As winter rages its private war within you, it becomes my touchstone, my silent apology, my gathering spot for what may lie ahead. Every morning, I place two fingers on it and take a deep breath.

Through it all, the trees maintain their sparkle. Until one night, we find you sitting on the cold, hard ground beneath their shadowy branches, trembling and afraid that all is lost. We cannot coax you back inside the house. From the window, I watch Daddy embrace you in a deep bear hug as you both slowly make your way up the driveway. I think again of your newborn self. I wondered if this darkness was inside the whole time – somewhere deep within your spirit.

Things do get better, little one.

We have lunch at a local café so often that the manager takes to pressing giant cookies into your palm while we sit at the table. Sometimes, we are silent over sandwiches. Sometimes, you talk and talk – as though there isn't enough time to say the words. One time, you walk out mid-meal, frustrated by how much I press you.

I don't mean to hover or push. But my mother's heart is shaken. No matter how hard I try to back off and give you space, I can't help but take your emotional pulse.

As the snow melts and the grass stands straight again, slowly, your spark returns. There is no magic to the healing beyond the basics – sleep, food, and time. You see, heartache demands we address our most primal needs first; it is rarely undone overnight.

One spring afternoon, I peer out the window. I see a silhouette on a ladder. The air is aglow with the breath and blaze of a hundred lights amongst branches, strung by a dark-haired boy trying to find his way. Now, with a new sky as his backdrop, he lifts strand after strand and coils them together over one arm. He drops them into the box at his feet – winter's stars gone silent.

And I think to myself: he is here, they are here, we are here.

We are afloat. For one more day, we are afloat.

For all your kite-cloud chasing, you make your way back home.

For now, we are out of the woods.

Yet I will never forget the trees.

My son, your future is bright.

Rest now, sweet baby, for you have much ahead of you in this one and only life you'll call yours.

Dark chocolate. That's the color of your eyes.

9

THE WHOLE CHILD – IT'S NOT ALWAYS ABOUT THE IEP TABLE

"WHAT SHOULD I ask for in our IEP meeting next week?"

Sweet Mama, your face was so earnest. I wanted to hug you.

I could feel your determination radiating off of you.

"Do you think he needs more speech therapy?"

Desperately, I wanted to give you the answer you longed to hear – that, yes, extra time with the speech therapist and more goals added to the already long list will transform your little boy.

The truth is, there wasn't one particular therapy or service that helped get Jack to where he is today.

Like you, I once pinned all my hopes on the conference room and the sheaf of papers that I clutched in my hands. But it doesn't work that way.

You are trying to raise a whole child.

A child who can forgive, and order in a restaurant, and cheer someone up after a bad day.

One who can sit in church, or his brother's baseball game, or through brunch at a fancy-ish restaurant.

A whole child doesn't spring out of a conference table or leap off of a page covered in black-and-white goals.

You and your partner each have a role to play in your new familial landscape. You have to let him play it, even if it's different than yours.

In other words, resist becoming The Person.

I did pretty well for the first year I was a mother. Our oldest son, Joey, was born, and, for the most part, my husband Joe and I handled the responsibility of taking care of a new baby fairly equally.

I didn't care how he swaddled him, which outfit he chose, or whether he used the blue pacifier with the duck on it or the green one with the frog when Joey fussed.

Then, Jack was born. He was a little, uh, *unusual* right from the beginning. He never looked at us, he never slept, and he cried all the time. Both Joe and I saw it – and we both worried.

We exchanged uneasy glances on the couch late at night while we took turns rocking, soothing, and walking our angry, mysterious baby.

Then, he was diagnosed with autism. And things changed.

We didn't sit together on the couch as much. We didn't exchange the glances, and we didn't take turns soothing. I think this was because, overnight, I became The Person.

After the diagnosis, I was the only person who could feed Jack the mashed bananas that he spit right back out at me. Only I could rock him to sleep so he would wake up twenty minutes later screaming. I knew just what kind of juice he preferred.

I threw myself headfirst into specialists. I read articles. I researched therapy. I was frantic – yet I thought I was the only one who understood him.

There I sat, on my island of invented expertise, like a carping queen in her ivory castle.

I took Jack right along with me. We looked around, and we looked at each other. We looked across a wide, deep spectrum moat that separated us and saw all the other people out there, having fun, laughing, and sitting in the sun.

This was not good – for me, Jack, or our marriage.

See, when you are the only one who can do everything – and you do it perfectly, and you sneer and roll your eyes when someone else tries to step in and help – then you will wind up doing every single thing yourself. And this will make you mad. A little sad too, but mostly mad.

Because if you are anything like me, you will blame your husband since, clearly, he is very lazy. He is maybe even a little bit stupid because he doesn't understand that the special diaper cream *must* go on every time this little hiney gets changed. And, if the bananas have any lumps, then it won't work. And the green bowl is really best because the bottom is flatter.

You blame and blame, and maybe you feel resentful. Resentfulness is like a tiny seed that plants itself in your heart and your mind. Instead of blossoming into a beautiful, silky flower, it grows into an ugly weed when you most need colorful petals.

This was me.

I bought the special diaper cream because I obviously cared about our son the most.

I mashed the bananas in the green bowl.

I sneered. I rolled my eyes.

And then we almost got divorced.

I am not kidding about this.

Back then, I thought it all mattered so much. I felt that if I didn't do everything exactly right, Jack wouldn't outgrow his autism, and our life would be miserable. That's what the voices in my head told me, anyway.

Well, we were pretty miserable, but it wasn't because of his autism. It was because I was trying to control my life's unfamiliar landscape through ridiculous details.

It was because Joe's opinion ceased to matter.

It was because I was alone, angry, and sad on my island, and I didn't even know how I got there.

People like me . . . we use smugness and sneering and bananas to protect a small inner light. This light – it flickers like a candle on a windy day.

The wind is trying to control our vulnerability and make it disappear. Vulnerability is scary. It makes us feel weak and cold and alone. It makes us feel defenseless.

We build a wobbly fortress around our candle out of sticks, stones, and green plastic bowls. We hide it from the wind, the world, and maybe even ourselves.

With my marriage crumbling before me, one stick at a time, I dismantled my fortress. I tried to weed out the resentment.

The truth is, when it comes to this unusual boy of ours, Joe is much better at many things than I am.

When they go grocery shopping, he always shows him the receipt so Jack can see that apples were on sale, but the grapes were more expensive than usual.

And when Jack is tired or he has a headache, it is his father he seeks. He stretches his long body on top of Joe's and closes his eyes.

He is the gain to my loss – the ultimate balance sheet of marriage and parenting.

I can't lie. Every now and again, the old voice in my head starts to whisper, and I fight the urge to become The Person again. I read the latest research on autism and begin to panic, or I worry Joe won't remember to give Jack his medicine when I'm out with my book club, and maybe I should write down a little reminder,

He always remembers.

Do me a favor. Take a moment today and look in the mirror. Look yourself right in right in the eye. Are you The Person? Are you standing in the way of a loving, messy, unpredictable relationship because you have marooned yourself on an ivory island?

The wind will stop blowing, I promise. You will stand straight, tall, and honest in the still, tranquil air. Nothing terrible will happen to any of you. It is in the quiet space of light where life is lived best.

Together, you will move away from the stuffy conference room and into the sunshine.

From there, teach this child everything you can think of to teach.

Teach him to bring the garbage cans in at night and to throw a load of towels in the wash.

Teach him how to dial 9-1-1 in an emergency and the way out of the house in case of a fire.

And on your most challenging days, when autism has stolen the very air you breathe, love him through it.

What if all we had to do was love our children?

Love them through their mistakes, their poor judgment, and their outbursts?

Their vulnerabilities. Their moods. Their highs and lows.

For eighteen years, doctors and therapists have told me what to do.

Use social stories, try medication, redirect his obsessions.

No one ever told me to simply love him.

Love the way his hair smells after a bath.

Love the way his chubby fingers grip a pencil.

Love how carefully he stacks his pillows at bedtime.

Love him through it.

Love him through this diagnosis that will follow him forever, like ants at a picnic.

Love him when anxiety clutches his spirit and smile.

Love him through his veneer of shame and embarrassment.

What if we loved our kids through spilled milk, bad report cards, and middle school?

I don't mean butterflies-rainbows-cliché kind of love. I mean the gritty, raw, tender kind.

The kind that requires us to listen, hear, try, and hurt.

What if we made our home the safest of spaces?

What if, during puberty, we bought special treats at the grocery store, made beds smooth with blankets, and lit candles during dinner?

It could work.

It could help our budding teens exhale. It could help smooth the jagged edges of their hormones, acne, and furiously changing bodies.

Inside, they are wilting flowers upon a fragile vine.

Inside, they need us even as they stubbornly push us away.

This boy, Jack, has lived under a magnifying glass for his entire life.

For as long as I can remember, his very existence has been quantified in terms of how many hours he slept, how he sat in his chair, and how often he made eye contact.

What if we measured it by smiles?

Jack has autism. He also has severe anxiety and obsessive-compulsive disorder.

You can't discipline any of this out of him. I know because I tried.

I tried telling him to stop being afraid of the wind chill factor. It didn't work.

I tried taking his beloved nightly Scooby Doo episodes away when he couldn't sit for circle time at school. It didn't work.

We need to love them through it.

One time, the school called. Jack was in sixth grade – a time when anxiety had taken a deep hold of him and manifested itself in his behavior. In other words, he kicked, screamed, cried, and bit his way through the day.

When we hung up, I was so frustrated, worried, aggravated, tired, and lost that I wanted to jump up and down and scream.

I wanted to believe he understood. I wanted to believe he knew the relationship between behavior and outcome – the familiar narrative that if I do A, then B will happen.

He didn't.

In the instant before I threw my phone against the wall, I realized.

I have to love him through it.

This would be my hardest work yet.

When my heart leans toward admonishing, I'll remind him he is enough.

When my thoughts veer toward frustration, I'll choose a gentle voice.

Inside and out, I will root for him.

After all, I've never once heard a mother say she looked back on her life and wished she had yelled more.

I've never heard anyone say they were glad they traded Scooby Doo for a seat in a circle.

Today, I will love him through this.

Looking back, I'm scared there are moments when I forgot.

When I saw the diagnosis before the boy.

When I reached for the towel before smelling his bath-time scent.

When I told him to stop, stop worrying and pacing.

Earnest Mama. Today, forget the IEP table. Set the magnifying glass aside.

Who knows, maybe you'll find the light no one else can find.

You are enough.

We are enough.

It's never really about the bananas.

Chocolate chip cookies. That's what Jack bakes when his dad has a bad day.

10

THIS IS MARRIAGE

THOUGH IT WILL LIKELY WIND up somewhere in the middle of the book, I wrote this chapter last. It seems fitting since we've always done things a little out of order.

We kissed before we held hands.

We found love before friendship.

I have so much to say, yet I am unsure where to begin. Taking something as big and expansive as a marriage and cramming it into a few thousand words *feels impossible*.

We met in a grimy kitchen. The air was heavy with the smell of French fries and deep-dish pizza. Pizzeria Uno's in June of 1994. I heard your voice before I saw your face, obscured as you were behind the stainless steel partition of a window full of food.

From there, a homecooked meal in your apartment. You made chicken stir fry. I was deeply touched to see you chopped all the vegetables ahead of time and stored them in small Ziplock bags – carrots, peppers, tiny florets of broccoli.

Like an arrow aimed toward a target, you knew you wanted to be a dentist. I was less sure of my future – dabbling in political science and literature and eventually (for reasons still unclear to me), landing on public policy. Let's just say you are the only one who wound up putting their degree to good use.

As summer leaves turned golden, we meandered together through a sunlit campus mainly made of stone archways and concrete stairwells. It was dominated by a large fountain at its center. You carried my books. Empty-handed, I turned to see your eyes in the yellow light.

The next ten years passed by like a slideshow.

One slide shows a sapphire ring with little white diamonds . . . offered after an argument in a tiny apartment.

A white dress and a black tuxedo in a small town church.

Graduations, with diplomas held aloft. New jobs – you in scrubs, me in pencil skirts and blazers. A brick house on a tree-lined street, both of us armed with paintbrushes and color swatches.

Snow. *So much snow* in this city of light.

Kentucky Fried Chicken in bed one sweltering Fourth of July, as the bedroom was the only air-conditioned space. We passed the bucket between us as fireworks boomed in the distance.

Posing with a newborn in the hospital, all tired eyes and relieved smiles.

The images are punctuated by outbursts and arguments as we attempt to tie our stories together. Story-tying is hard work. There is no manual for it. Our dynamic is established immediately – loud, explosive arguments followed by quiet and, eventually, grace. This is the marital music to which we dance.

Yet, for the most part, the decade is smooth. From 1994 – 2004, life felt manageable.

Before we got married, we did something called Pre-Cana. It was a preparation course our church recommended. Sitting in another couple's living room while their dark-haired toddler scooted around our feet, we answered questions about how we'd spend the holidays, how we'd handle a budget, and where we'd like to live.

No one asked what it would be like to have a special-needs child.

A child who never sleeps, runs away every chance he has, screams swear words at the top of his lungs, struggles to make sense of the social landscape, takes medicine every day, and gets suspended in middle school.

Who – at 6'5" – would reach for your hand in the parking lot, no matter the stares.

Would it have mattered? No. Probably not. But maybe it would have lodged something tiny and flickering in our subconscious. Perhaps we would've been more prepared for a formal diagnosis and all it might mean for us.

Now, at night, we sit together on the couch. Me, with my laptop, you with the remote.

The couches have changed over the years. First, it was white with an embroidered design. In our apartment, you stood over the sewing machine, piecing together long strips of fabric. You finished the cushions and sewed the rest by hand, using a running stitch taken from your book on oral surgery. Once it was done, we had a Couch Party to celebrate.

From there, a tan microfiber sofa – chosen for its durability and crumb-masking. Next, a deep red sectional, now relegated to the basement in favor of today's slate blue. You made coconut shrimp.

If we were so inclined, our entire family history can be traced back to fabric and cushions. Although the styles have changed, the symbolic nature of this piece of furniture remains consistent. It is our command center, our battleground, our comfort zone.

In the beginning, we stretched out under blankets, a cozy fire in the fireplace . . . watching endless television in our small living room. The X-Files, The Sopranos on VHS tapes, Rocky I and II.

Then we rocked fussy infants. We held feverish toddlers. We watched shows with middle-schoolers. America's Got Talent, Twenty-Five Words or Less, the Buffalo Bills, and the Yankees.

Now, we wait for headlights to make a slow sweep up the driveway – another teenage driver home safe.

We nudge tweens from their rooms, luring them from their nests with popcorn. Rose sits on the end nearest you while Henry favors a pillow on the floor.

We exchange nervous glances as we watch out the window for Charlie to finish the last of the Christmas lights, strung together between moments of panic and despair.

We argue and wonder about the next step for Jack. Our voices take on a familiar jagged edge, honed and sharpened over time. He pops his head into the room every few minutes, forever in tune with our escalating nervous systems.

A few days ago, we had a terrible argument.

We sat facing one another, shouting. I was angry and frustrated. And at the same time, I wanted nothing more than for you to fold me in your arms.

I can hardly remember what started it in the first place. It was about everything and nothing. Teenagers, money, autism. What can I say? The clutter of life wears us down sometimes.

We didn't talk the following day. I hate this. So many things happened, but I couldn't tell you because I was teaching you a good lesson about how right I was.

A squirrel got his head stuck in the bird feeder, the UPS guy ran over a package on his way down the driveway, and I heard an old song we both love.

It was as though none of it happened at all. Not the silly squirrel or the package or the song. Nothing is real until I tell it to you.

As we edge closer to our twenty-fourth wedding anniversary, I consider all the ways we've changed. There are many versions of marriage within two decades. Wide-eyed newlyweds, worn-down parents, terrified advocates.

Slowly but surely, we are making our way into yet another season. Reading glasses. A beautiful silver threading through your dark hair. Laugh lines appear out of smoothness.

You seem ready for it. I am not. I want to hold onto our younger selves for just a while longer. Perhaps this is vanity speaking. Maybe it is another language entirely – the language of immortality. I need to live forever. There is too much at stake in my absence.

A young mother once asked me how I made sure I paid enough attention to all of our kids. Her face was so earnest, open, and honest; I wanted to hug her. For a split second, I considered listing strategies for emotional child management in a larger family when another thought popped into my head entirely.

"Worry less about the attention you give your kids," I told her, "And more about the attention you give your marriage."

From there, our conversation took a wildly different turn. Marriage counseling. Date nights carved out in the busy weekly schedule. How to be okay with going to bed angry so you may wake prepared to forgive in the morning.

These are things we did – without shame or regret. Once a week in a somewhat small room, we perched on the edge of our armchairs and confessed our rage, our petty slights, and our bewilderment while a kindly gentleman in glasses nodded and soothed.

We untangled our familial baggage and made plans for better communication. We healed.

Perhaps the greatest gift from our time in this room was his gentle words at the end of each session, spoken softly as he opened the door and released us into the evening air.

"Remember, you love each other."

Now, I notice the small things. The way you offer me the first bite of every meal. How you reach for my hand in a crowd. Silly texts throughout the day.

The time we were watching a movie, and I said I was hungry because I didn't get a chance to eat much during dinner. Without a word, you got up and went into the kitchen. You took out a pan and put the toaster on the counter. You scrambled eggs and buttered toast. It was perhaps one of the tastiest meals I'd eaten in a long time.

Lately, when it comes to Jack and autism, we are not – as they say – on the same page. This isn't the first time.

Typically, I latch onto an idea – integrated preschool, music therapy – and you don't say much. You nod your head, and I take that as agreement. I throw myself headlong into the research and the cost. Then I present both to you.

Except we aren't talking about preschool or learning to play the recorder.

We're talking about a college experience. We're talking about the first tentative steps toward independence.

As usual, you kept your concern to yourself. As a father to this boy, this is what you do. You nod, you think, you consider every angle.

A father's grief is a private, internal affair. It takes place after hours – when I take my leave from the colors of the couch and head to bed.

A mother's grief, on the other hand, is loud. It fills the room. It demands oxygen.

Yours is private and internal.

You and I have what's called an Autism Marriage.

An Autism Marriage is amplified.

It's like someone held up a magnifying glass and blew up all our faults, weaknesses, and problems. It made us impossibly human.

You taught Jack how to grill burgers, hang Christmas lights, shovel the driveway, and pray in church.

I did homework. I helped him answer the phone and watch a boiling pot on the stove.

These were our roles. We did what came naturally to us.

We thought we were over the hump, didn't we? We both thought the worst was behind us. We got through puberty, a new school, and changes in medication.

And now, this next step is upon us.

I thought we were on the same page.

But I watched your face and wide eyes – and for the first time, I realized just how terrified you are to let him go. I am, too. I think we're just terrified of different things.

When it comes to our vulnerable son, your worries are outward, while mine are matters of the heart. Loneliness and rejection hover around my periphery.

I'm afraid he won't meet people, and you're worried he'll meet the wrong people.

You think about him crossing the street, walking to campus alone, being out at night.

I know your heart without words, without conversation.

Autism is forever. It will never be behind us. We know this, yet lately, it seems you and I are unwilling to stretch our hands to the fire and feel the heat of our imminent future.

Still, we root for him.

We root for the underdog.

We root for the boy who doesn't always have a voice of his own.

A specific worry accompanies launching a vulnerable child into the world.

For seventeen years, we have interpreted this boy to the world and this world to the boy, yet the question lingers in the air like smoke from a campfire.

Have we done enough?

Have we explained and advocated and hoped and hurt and tried enough?

Maybe.

Maybe not.

All day long, we push uphill. We work to speak autism's language. And once we master a few sentences, we turn around and offer the words.

No one believes in him the way we do. That's the thing.

His first word was *ball*. He was three years old. He said it as though he'd been storing it up for all his little life.

They see *autism*, and the idea of a college experience seems ridiculous.

It's not ridiculous. Together, we will get him there. Wherever that is.

When it comes to autism, you were always the rule-breaker.

You never asked *why*.

Instead, you asked *why not*.

You both are very different.

Your love language is food and affection.

He resists an embrace. He loathes anything chewy, mixed together, or spicy.

You are the man with an easy smile; he is the boy who rarely laughs at all.

You are very different, yes, but also similar.

You share the same furrowed brow, a fondness for cookies, and a tendency to keep your heads down when you walk.

For as long as I can remember, you have had a unique tendency to elevate each other. One of you gets loud and agitated, and the other follows – a nervous system game of cat-and-mouse.

It makes me anxious. I hate it. I used to try and manage you both. Your moods, interactions, arguments, and opinions. This was perhaps my most unanticipated aspect of motherhood. In my mind, the three letters of my maternal namesake are also an acronym. M.O.M. – otherwise known as Manager of Moods.

See, when you have a diagnosed child, there is a triangle of sorts: mother, father, boy. Firmly, we sit in our angled corners, convinced we know the best way. Our way.

Then, one day, I simply let go. I stopped trying to be the safety net upon which you fell, breathless, irritated, and divided.

I remember the exact moment: Jack was fourteen. We were at a middle school concert with plans to go out for dinner afterward. It was early March. The metal sky spit a cold rain.

Jack didn't want to be there. He fidgeted while the singers performed. At one point, he looked straight at you and shouted the worst swear word he could. You stood up angrily and steered him toward the door. A folding chair clattered to the floor as you moved.

My inclination was to follow – to soothe and mediate.

But I didn't. I stayed and watched the next song, then the next. I was tired of being in the middle.

That was four years ago.

At times, watching you together is like watching a chaotic dance. You seem out of sync, out of rhythm.

But I can only play observer to your most intense moments. As much as I hate it, I believe my downshifted role helped you establish and re-establish who you are to one another.

Chasing father, racing son.

In other words, I was standing in the way of this beautifully messy relationship.

Slowly, like a painting under the artist's brush, you have emerged vibrant with color. You found each other. The sharp angles didn't disappear altogether, but they became smoother. Softer. Something closer to a circle than a triangle.

My husband, you are my witness.

And I yours.

We are witness to all the ways we help him claim the piece of earth that is rightfully his. Side by side, we stand firmly rooted to the ground. We stretch our gaze toward the sky.

And on the days when it was all too much for me, when I couldn't see the sun for the clouds or take another step in the name of spectrum progress, you took my hand in yours and helped me reach beyond the storm.

You held up half my sky.

Now, let me do the same for you.

He is ready. In my heart, I believe this.

I know we are not on the same page right now.

Still, I choose you.

I choose you when it's hard – when we stand on opposite sides of the spectrum's wide divide.

We will move mountains for him.

It might simply be different mountains.

Maybe there is no perfect answer. There is just me, you, this boy, and autism.

Rooting for the underdog is equal parts thrilling/scary/ordinary/new.

At the end of the day, I guess all we can do is hope the world is gentle.

For years, he held your hand. Now, he walks beside you. Together, you share the same stride.

You did this.

You taught him to reach, yes.

You also taught him how to stand on his own.

In the slideshow of our life, one memory has the strongest foothold in my mind – stronger, even, than the white dress and the fireworks.

Outside a middle school, two silhouettes stand beneath a raw March sky. They sway together in the dusky light – as if to music only they can hear.

Tender father.

And the boy who ran before he walked.

Ball was his first word.

Daddy was his second.

You hold up half my sky.

True Companion by Marc Cohen. That's what came on the radio. Our wedding song.

Two thousand nine hundred and ten words. I could have written forever more.

11

OF MICE AND MEN

ONCE UPON A TIME, coal miners released canaries into the mine shafts to test the air quality and oxygen levels. Known for their gift of song, these small birds are much more sensitive than humans to the deadly carbon monoxide found underground.

They carried them down in special cages. Once inside, they would open the door and listen for the delicate melody.

A sudden halt in the music would warn workers to evacuate the pit. The coal miners would rescue the birds by closing the cage door and opening a valve to pump oxygen inside.

When I first heard this, I thought of you.

My daughter.

But I am getting ahead of myself.

Where should I begin?

At the beginning, I guess.

A dining room in an old house in Buffalo. The kind with rich, dark woodwork, lots of wallpaper, and a small kitchen.

It was March. Our neighbors had invited us to a dinner party. Every guest was at least forty years our senior – and one of the men kept calling me *Kristy*. Over our crystal stemware and white plates, Daddy and I exchanged stolen smiles.

I sat at the table with my arms folded against my pregnant belly. As we ate, we bantered about names, about gender.

I claimed to make only boys, referencing the three brothers who came before you. I confessed to having no names. Daddy wanted Drew, or maybe James. We hadn't really talked much about what to name a girl . . . other than your father favored long, Italian ones like Francesca or Isabella.

The truth is, I couldn't imagine having a daughter. The idea of pink mixed up with all that blueness confounded me.

As the hostess cleared the dishes and cut slices of pie, one of the wives leaned close to me.

"If the baby is a girl, name her Rose. You can buy her roses on her birthday."

Rose. Of course. I turned it around in my mind until it settled just right.

It was Daddy's late grandmother's name. Nonna Rose was what everyone called her. I knew it would fit nicely inside the idea of legacy, of heritage. But the truth is, I first discovered it surrounded by neighbors and papered walls.

The rest of the pregnancy was mostly uneventful, until the last month when your head was still up, in the breech position. Convinced he could nudge you into the proper position, my doctor performed what's called a *version*. For half an hour, I lay on a hospital bed with my body at a slight incline and my head elevated, hoping you might drift further down. Then, all giant hands and jovial nature, he massaged my huge stomach and coaxed you around until your head was facing the exit door, so to speak. It didn't hurt a bit.

A few weeks later, you arrived on a warm morning in July. A girl. At nine pounds, four ounces, you edged Jack out by a single ounce. The labor and delivery nurse joked that Daddy was so shocked she could have tipped him over with her finger.

Now, fourteen years later, I sit beside you on your bed. The room itself has gone through many iterations. Soft pink with an accent wall. Daddy measured out the stripes and carefully painted them a darker hue. Your grandmother made the window treatments – rosy flowers against a cream background.

From there, a light green. Now, a shade of turquoise with coral accents. We picked out the pillows while your friends giggled in the aisle. You stood, un-giggly. Giggling was never your style. Your joy is private.

At this moment, you are stretched out on top of the covers – all six feet of you. Your face is down in the pillow, your wildly curly hair fanned all around you. You are inconsolable.

Of Mice and Men.

How did I forget they showed this movie in ninth grade?

I did, though. I forgot how your brothers struggled to understand the plot while a classroom full of kids absorbed the story as if it were nothing. I forgot to call the office and have you excused.

I smooth your curls with my hands. I know it's not enough, but it's all you'll allow.

My birdie, my canary, my daughter wrapped in yellow. You have so little armor.

Written in 1937 by John Steinbeck, Of Mice and Men is set against the backdrop of the Great Depression. Two migrant workers, George and Lennie, wander the United States searching for jobs. Lennie depends on George. He is depicted as simple and largely misunderstood.

At one point, Lennie is accused of an act of violence. George tries to cover.

You flip over and stare at the ceiling. Tears slide down your face.

I attempt to calm you by having you focus on your surroundings – getting out of your mind and into your body. I suggest you relax your palms and feel the comforter between your fingers. Lower your shoulders away from your ears, and take deep breaths in through the nose, out through your mouth. For a moment, it works.

As we dissect the story, layering it against our own, I try to weed out fact versus feeling, even as my own heart vibrates.

Yes, Lennie is described as tall, like Jack. He asks the same questions over and over, even when he knows the answers, like Jack. He is vulnerable and misunderstood.

"What do we know for sure?" I ask you. This is a regular question in our house. It's a way to establish the truth – to ground us in reality.

It is not 1937. A lot has changed since then.

Jack has an official diagnosis.

He has an IEP and a team of therapists and teachers.

He has a family. Brothers, a sister, a multitude of cousins. People who will watch for him for the rest of his life.

Jack is not Lennie.

Since you were a tiny girl, you've always connected deeply to him. You feel his pulse as your own.

Sure, it was cute at first. Endearing. You nicknamed him "Jackie." You were the only one who called him that.

In first grade, you came home crying. Jack was in fourth grade. You rode the same bus back and forth to school. You noticed he always sat alone. He never talked to any other kids.

When he struggled in sixth grade, you crocheted bracelets made of yarn. The Easter Bunny delivered the hook and multicolored strands. Alone in your room, you threaded long braids. In the morning, before school, you told him to pull them between his fingers whenever he felt anxious or worried. He wore them around his wrist for the better part of a year.

One night, over egg rolls and lo mein in a restaurant with black lacquered chairs, you listened patiently as he looped about the fire drill at school. You were perhaps eight years old. This was when your hair was straight, and you wore it in a bob. It was the sweetest haircut.

Last year, it was a movie about bullying. A teenager had committed suicide when his peers relentlessly called him strange and weird. You slept in our room for a week.

It is real to you.

My daughter, it is real to me, too.

The weight is growing heavier. I long to tell you to set it down, but I know you won't. Sisterhood is built into your DNA the same way rigidity and anxiety are built into his.

I never meant for you to carry it in the first place. Somehow, when no one was looking, you slipped your shoulders beneath autism's weight.

The next morning, you sit at the kitchen island eating breakfast. Wordless, you gather your things and follow Charlie to the car.

We always say the world is not made for people like Jack.

I wonder if it's not made for the brothers or sisters either – the songbirds who alter their own music again and again – without any choice in the matter whatsoever.

I watch you walk out the door, your shoulders squared and your head high. I ache for you. Just before you leave, you turn back and look at me.

"Will anyone ever know him for who he is?"

Rose Isabella.

Remember your own oxygen valve, your own air.

Jack is not Lennie.

Jack is not Lennie.

He has a family.

He has a sister.

12

WE BEGAN AS ENEMIES

WE BEGAN AS ENEMIES.

It was November 2005. I was standing with a little boy in a parking garage. He was eighteen months old. The words from the doctor were still ringing in my ears.

"Mrs. Cariello, I believe your son has Autism Spectrum Disorder."

At first, we had no idea. He was just a chubby, squirming baby who rarely slept. He cried more than we expected.

Slowly, you made your presence known.

The sleep got worse.

The cries got louder.

The quiet got quieter.

You were sick constantly in the beginning. Acid reflux, ear infections, and a deep, barking cough. We blamed daycare and its carpet full of germs. I added *working mother* to the long list of things that made me feel guilty.

Still, I charged full steam ahead.

I spent my lunch hour scouring the Internet for information — lists of symptoms, suggestions for speech, and possible therapies to help with the outbursts that now punctuated our days. Anything to give me purchase as I began this long uphill climb on what was proving to be a very slippery slope.

I wanted to read about you. I was desperate for research. Maybe sign language was the answer . . . or integrated preschool. Music class.

Joe took the wait-and-see approach. He wanted to slow down and understand you.

I was right; he was wrong. He was right; I was wrong.

I was frantic.

He was methodical.

I was raw.

He was angry.

Because of you, we were both lost.

Oh sure, we never fought about you *specifically*. Instead, we fought over who got more sleep, who spent more money, and who did more housework, all while a wolf knocked quietly at the door — an interloper in the dark of the night.

Inside every marriage is a secret language. A private code of nicknames and jokes and memories.

The days are full of a thousand tiny hurts, followed by a million small recoveries. And once you bared your long, yellow teeth in our house, the jokes ebbed. Our nicknames faded, and our attempts at recovery were dwarfed by the hurt.

Because of you, our young marital ground was sliding beneath us, and separately, we each battled the nagging feeling that the landscape of our little family was shifting for good. We were a statistic, a number, a plot line on the spectrum's sloping bell curve.

You and I are like two boxers in a ring, circling and jabbing. We attempt to gain whatever we can against each other.

We are brother and sister at the end of a long, hot car ride, poking, needling, annoying, and griping.

We are the quintessential cat-and-mouse. We take our turns chasing and hiding, hiding and chasing.

I am always watching you to see what move you'll make next.

And like a stray cat in the dark, you are always waiting for me to give up or get tired.

I will never get tired.

You are the panther who demands Melatonin for six hours of sleep at night.

You are the cruel snake of anxiety, winding and curling around my child's soul.

You are the box on a form, a bad day at school, marital discord, and a mother's uncertainty.

I hate you.

That's right, I said it. Autism, I hate you.

I hate how lonely you make him.

I hate the way he painstakingly searches for words while the rest of the world rushes over him – a tidal wave of jokes and irony and dialogue and poetry.

I hate that his brain is always turning, churning, obsessing, racing from maps to music to when Smucker's first made strawberry jam. I want to scream at you to leave my son alone. Let him rest for a moment.

Please, let him rest.

I hate the way you make him feel. Because of you, he is insecure and alone.

I hate the way you make me feel. With you around, I am stupid and tired and useless.

In the beginning, I suppose I wanted the same things for him as everyone else. I wanted a report card with more A's than C's. I wanted soccer games on Saturday mornings and a shiny black tux for the prom.

Over time, I learned to want different things: a small smile, a day without a phone call from school, and an easy evening.

That little boy, Jack, from the parking lot, is nearly eighteen now. In two days, we will stand in a courtroom and apply for guardianship according to New Hampshire family law.

Weeks ago, we sat at the table and filled out the paperwork. We listed all the specific ways our son has demonstrated an inability to navigate aspects of his own life.

Jack will sit with his state-appointed lawyer at one table while Joe and I sit at another. Before a judge, our attorney will make a case for why we must remain in charge of his finances and health care.

I fear this may break him.

How did it come to this?

This is your fault.

Or is it?

One moment, I believe this is true. The next doubt creeps in like a stray cat on the back steps.

Did we do enough?

He can wash and fold his own laundry. He can use the grill to make cheeseburgers. He manages the family grocery list and remembers to call his grandfather on his birthday.

But he gives out too much personal information. He thinks cars cost $500. He can't comprehend the concept of a mortgage.

He is naïve.

He is clever.

He is earnest.

His body resembles a man's, while his spirit delights in the online app for Pizza Hut.

When it comes to autism, you can't take your eye off the ball for one single second. You can't loosen your grip on the goals or try to walk instead of chase. Autism is the lens through which life is sharpened and clarified.

You have been around since the beginning of time, despite the façade of "normal" assembled by generations before us.

Musicians, painters, inventors, creators. You have influenced them all.

Mozart wrote long, complicated symphonies. His hearing was rumored to be so sensitive he could hear the difference in the slightest tone. His concentration was so fierce that he would skip meals for days to finish a piece.

Historians explain how Michelangelo made sketch after sketch until the final pose was perfect in his rigid, unbending mind. Because of you, the Sistine Chapel explodes with light and color.

Records show that Albert Einstein did terribly in school. He didn't learn the same way as all the other kids. Yet his brilliance changed the world.

And Sir Isaac Newton of the fallen apple had no friends. He didn't understand people, and he insisted on a strict, unwavering routine.

You see, a still mind can still have great thoughts; within even the quietest person, there is a voice. A painting, a song.

You are music and dreams, kindness and color. You are gravity.

I should be proud, right? I should be honored to have my son join the diagnostic reputation of such influential people.

Yet I tire of the success stories. I am drained by the propaganda. This is not our experience. It is not his kind of autism.

People ask me all the time what kind he has. Is he high verbal? High functioning? Maybe a savant?

Yes, maybe, no.

He isn't a savant. He doesn't swirl colorful blobs of paint into a masterpiece. He doesn't play virtuosos on the piano or recite long mathematic equations.

He sleeps with six pillows and one weighted blanket.

He is profoundly anxious and unapologetically honest.

He wants the same things for himself that everyone else enjoys.

The chance to drive down the street, the experience of falling in love, a life of independence.

This is the kind of autism my son has. It's the kind that is stingy with accomplishments and rich in fear.

It's the kind that knows the difference between who he is and who he is not.

It is the breaking kind.

Hope. We clutch it between our palms like an invisible answer.

Every once in a while, I wonder what the world would be like if everyone had the chance to raise a child like Jack.

Politicians.

School principals.

Neurologists, jet pilots, the woman at the gym who loudly complains her son didn't get into an Ivy League college.

What would the world look like?

These are the questions I ask myself as I lie awake in the darkness of my bedroom, wondering what the future looks like for this boy of mine.

I promise I say this without bitterness or spite. I am genuinely curious.

What would change?

Our barometer for success? Certainly.

Maybe we'd have more self-driving cars.

Maybe we'd all be apologetically honest once in a while.

I guess we'll never know.

I think behind our wildly beating hearts is a song.

This song . . . well, it is our story of pork chops for dinner, the rare teenage smile, and pillows at bedtime.

It is the by-product of building a family.

For many years, I thought my story was about a boy and his autism.

Perhaps it is simply the melody of every mother, spelled out on paper – the fierce hope, loneliness, and fragments of joy we fearlessly bundle into each and every day.

Autism is my permanent lens; it's true.

Yet, there are the briefest moments when autism ceases to be the center of it all. And in the space of exactly one breath, I can see this boy Jack for exactly who he is.

I glimpse his pureness, his sincerity, and his spirit.

Autism, let me tell you a secret.

I know you think you keep all the secrets, but I also have one: every once in a while, when I'm frustrated and lost, I go up into our bedroom, and I cry.

I sit in the chair by the window. I cry for the boy who wants to live alone but may not, who wants to drive a car to the grocery store for ice cream but can't, and who wants a purple velvet cake for his 18th birthday.

I cry for the boy who might have been.

I cry for the way he holds onto the hem of life's kite and watches the clouds race overhead.

He wishes for buoyancy and flight while you keep his feet planted firmly on the ground.

You see, in a culture obsessed with trophies, Ivy Leagues, ego, status, and wealth, you have robbed him of his currency.

We began as enemies in a cold November parking lot.

What are we now? I don't think there is a term for it, to be honest.

You are less enemy, but not friend.

I want to hate you, autism, but like a child picking petals from a flower, I vacillate between hate and love, loathing and tenderness.

To hate you would be to hate a fundamental piece of my Jack-a-boo, and that is something I can never ever do, no matter which way the silky petals scatter in the wind.

I know you love this boy almost as much as I do. In some ethereal way, I know you chose him – you chose me, and us.

Because of you, this dark-haired man and I found one another again. Amid diapers and speech therapy, doctor's visits, and long, sleepless nights, we rediscovered our private language.

And for all the things you make him – rigid, bossy, lonely, sad – you also make him funny, lovable, charming, and smart. In some absurd way, you make him whole. To love him is to love you, too.

You are a million little papercuts throughout the daily business of life – the small heartbreaks that accompany a complicated child.

You are the catch in my breath when I see another teenage boy bouncing a ball or flirting with a girl.

You are an uncertain future, a past full of regrets, a mother desperately trying to live in the moment.

At the same time, you are perspective.

You robbed him of his currency.

Or did you?

Did you simply alter the exchange? Did you simply open our eyes to a life full of things that truly matter?

A bittersweet season is upon us.

As I wrestle with the cold process of guardianship and all it may mean, I am coming to terms with a novel kind of independence: college.

In a few short months, this boy, Jack, will pack up his things and move into a residential space. It is geared for kids like him – kids who require structure and scaffolding to do what comes easily for most.

I don't know how to let him go.

Do you?

Can we loosen our grip – mine maternal, yours diagnostic – and let him fly?

We began as enemies.

I don't know what to call us now.

Every once in a while, I cry for the boy who might have been, it's true. But every single day, I smile for the boy who is. I smile for what is possible.

"For Mom. I think I want to take a class. In broadcasting."

Maybe the question isn't about *what kind* of autism he has.

Maybe it's how we surrendered to a life we didn't ask for, but we love all the same.

He doesn't even like strawberry jam.

13

THE LADY OF THE HOUSE

YOU ARE SPRING.

You are yellow daffodils poking through the cool soil. A newly planted garden. Palm Sunday, Easter dinner, Mother's Day in May.

The first time we met, you were standing at the stove stirring sauce. I was nineteen years old. I was in love with your son.

Right away, I noticed your accent. Of course, Joe had explained your history: the boat ride from Italy to America when you were sixteen, how you left your mother and sisters behind to keep house and cook for your brother and father in Brooklyn. You met your husband in an apartment adjacent to yours during a celebration for a baptism.

Being a daughter-in-law is weird. I think we can agree on that.

From the very beginning, the role was unfamiliar to me. Throughout my childhood, divorce was the oceanic current upon which our little family bobbed and swayed. It pulled us this way and that. In other words, in-laws were a short-term experience.

In all my recollections, I never once remember my mother interacting with my father's parents or vice-versa. I had no context. I didn't understand the expectations.

I once read a story about a woman who spread a beautiful tapestry across the floor. It was embroidered with vibrant flowers and swooping birds; it would be a unique tablecloth. She smoothed it carefully with both hands. She was about to meet her son's soon-to-be wife and wanted to make a good impression. She glanced at her table, bare and ready for all the special dishes she spent days preparing.

Her son walked through the door with his beloved. She saw the cloth lying across the floor. Eager to make her own good impression, she immediately stepped on it and wiped her feet. The older woman gasped. She looked back at her table and back down at the tablecloth, which was soiled and unusable.

It reminded me of us – reluctant daughter-in-law, confident mother-in-law.

In the beginning, I often stumbled upon whatever you offered – window treatments for our new apartment, a set of placemats, another pasta dish.

I think the food overwhelmed me. I was raised with portions. During dinner, we always made the exact servings for the number of people eating – four pork chops, four ears of corn, four plates set around the little wooden circle.

My family seemed so small; my traditions were swallowed up inside your big Italian heritage. You appeared intact and whole compared to my family's fissures.

Marriage did not come naturally to me. The models in my life had short endings, if you will. I never witnessed a union last more than five years. I was unprepared for the longevity.

I often carried my petty gripes to you like so many green apples in a pail. The way he grumbled about a new shower curtain, came home late for dinner, snored in bed at night.

And when children and autism made their way into our lives, I brought you our most jagged moments. I didn't know where else to turn. To you, I confessed the anger, the arguments, the tempers lost. You listened quietly as you stirred or hemmed or folded. You were perpetually in motion – a one-woman show of industry and hard work.

As I talked, you nodded. You were practical with your words. You reminded me people rarely change. You shared ways to circumvent the arguments – how to let some things go in the moment. It called to mind a movie quote that explains the man may be the head of the house, but the woman is the neck. She can turn the head however she likes.

Well, you raised him, I'd banter playfully.

But you married him, you'd counter, a sparkle in your eye.

Tell him, you advised. *You are the lady of the house.*

I've watched you sing infants to sleep, hem a skirt, and turn warm soil into a plump red tomato.

I've listened to you explain how every meal should start with soup, even in the middle of summer.

You have twenty grandchildren. Yet you marveled at each newborn as though you've never seen one before in your life. You admired the tiny hands, the ears shaped like seashells, the halo of silken hair.

Then came Jack. He was the seventeenth in a long line – and the first official diagnosis in the family.

Autism Spectrum Disorder.

It wasn't smooth at first. Desperately, you longed to know him. You just didn't know how. You worried about jackets in the rain and well-rounded meals with plenty of fresh vegetables.

Slowly, you forged your way. You figured each other out. You noticed his fondness for chocolate sandwich cookies and his angst in middle school. You learned that autism's thunderstorms quickly make way to sunshine.

For this, there is no jacket.

Every Sunday morning, you sat at the table peeling ripe yellow pears. Knife facing palm – which everyone knows is the most dangerous way to cut anything – you sliced them into pieces and passed them around the table. He delighted in each juicy bite. It was the only time I ever saw him enjoy fruit.

Time and time again, he brought you Bunny, the most precious of his belongings. The keeper of his sleep, the soother of anxiety, was the stuffed rabbit whose ears and tail were subject to fierce forefinger-and-thumb rubbing on the worst days. He's slept with it since the day he was born.

He brought Bunny for fixing. Without a word – not even a *tsk tsk* about why a teenager sleeps with a stuffed animal – you got up and went to the sewing machine in the basement. In the cool darkness, you repaired this boy's heartache by way of needle and thread.

Every year, you hosted his birthday dinner. Without friends, family was all he has. You blew up balloons, made the chicken cutlets he loved, and celebrated his turn around the sun.

IT IS SPRINGTIME NOW. Tiny green buds dot the trees. Beneath the ground, previously planted seeds begin stretching and expanding toward the light.

Yet this spring season is unlike the others.

You are sick. Acute Myeloid Leukemia — a deadly blood disease that began in the marrow of your bones.

I can't decide if the timing is ironic or exquisite, the way your last breath will see you through your favorite season, but likely not much beyond it. Is it a gift to have your final days also be the ones you love most, where the earth loses its frigid layer and begins to soak up the warmth?

Or is it frustrating not to participate fully in your part of shaping the landscape as you once did? Watering the flowers, shifting soil around, plucking stubborn weeds. To know, year after year, spring will come again despite your absence, as seasons have no loyalty.

I don't ask you any of this, though. Our visits are brief and abbreviated now. We save our words.

Since your diagnosis, there has been a flurry of activity. Trips into Boston to see the top specialist in the field. Discussions about trial treatments and outcomes and possibilities. One doctor thinks he has the right combination of therapy drugs and marrow transplants. He is confident he can extend your life, even if he can't predict for how long.

Your sons want it. Desperately, they want to save you. And who can blame them? Who can deny this fervent hope?

The women of the family are less sure.

As I observe from the sidelines, I can't help but think it would make an interesting gender study on grief. Men battle. They research and fight.

Women, on the other hand, know the failings of the body. We've had miscarriages, birthed children, fed newborns, kissed scraped knees. We understand fragility.

In the end, you made the final call. You decided you don't want to live at half-mast, like a boat with the sails only partly full of wind. You don't want a calendar full of appointments and transfusions. To me, it was perhaps the most graceful and courageous choice.

Late at night, we sit together, this dark-eyed man with a bit of silver threading through his wavy hair. His shoulders sag. He shields his eyes with his hand.

"I had the least amount of time with her," he murmurs.

As your youngest, this is technically true. And if there's anything this son of yours is good at, it's the technical part of life. He is logic over emotion, metrics instead of heartbeats. So he says, anyway.

I nod my head in agreement. Yes, he had the least amount of time with you. Yet because of motherhood's universal arc, he also had the gentlest version of you. We start out all straight spine and strictness, but by the last child, we are softer. The years of childrearing smooth out our edges.

How can the sun rise if you're not here to see it? This is what I ask myself as your garden goes untended.

Telling the kids was hard. Grief is a terrible part of life. It is pure sadness and despair. It's bad enough that grown-ups must endure it. Watching your children endure it is akin to feeling your skin on fire.

Research tells us people with autism have trouble forming meaningful connections.

Yet one afternoon, as Joe and I drove to the hospital after you were admitted with a fever, my phone vibrated. It was Jack.

"Can you tell Grandma this?"

"What, buddy?" I typed back.

"Grandma, I'm going to miss you. I realize for the past few days that Bunny is so fixed. Sunday mornings will not be the same and I have kept thinking about you every single day."

You always rooted for him. Even when you didn't quite understand diagnostic concepts of cognitive flexibility, executive functioning, and global delay. None of it mattered to you, anyway.

It's easy to assume rooting for someone is like being a cheerleader – all sparkly pom-poms and glittery applause.

It's not. It's quieter. It's gentle questions about school, stocking the pantry with Oreos, and never demanding a hug because hugs were sometimes more than this boy could give.

As sickness prevails and your body continues to weaken, I watch my husband tuck pillows behind your back. I watch as he wheels you to bed and arranges your covers just so. Despite a few sour apple moments, I've chosen my partner well.

This is your most precious gift – the gift of clearing away life's clutter so we can view what was right in front of us the whole time. There is great joy in the ordinary. A fresh tomato from the garden, a quick joke, a newborn's soft sigh.

Again and again, I saw my children through your eyes. Their triumphs, earnestness, and delightful ability to live precisely in the moment.

A few days ago, after a transfusion, you sat upright in your wheelchair. Your eyes had that familiar spark to them. Bolstered by fresh energy, you ordered your house back together via vacuum, Windex, and mop.

A rally, we fervently hope. *Maybe a corner turned or a reprieve from the vicious disease ravaging your body.*

Perhaps, though, it is nothing more than good old-fashioned practical sense. After all, if a bunch of people are about to drop by the house, it darn well better be clean.

This, in a nutshell, is you, my mother-in-law.

The glue of the family – the soup-maker, storyteller, Bunny-fixer.

Soon, you will be gone.

You will be gone, yet we'll still see you in the most unexpected places.

The fabric that frames our windows, silky curtains reaching the floor.

An errant Tupperware lid, leftover from a dish of ravioli pressed into our hands.

The lullaby before bedtime, the fresh bite of juicy pear, a tender patch of earth turned green.

You will go, and still, the sun will rise.

It will rise because it doesn't know what else to do.

It will rise because everything must come to an end, no matter how sad, broken, restless, or angry we are.

For now, we are all these things.

In time, we will understand. After all, even the darkest night ends with light.

Until then, we will remember the woman who cooked, loved, planted, and advised.

Forever the lady of her house.

You always had the loveliest tablecloths.

Bunny is fixed. Rest easy.

14

HELLO. GOODBYE.

DEAR ANXIETY,

I hate you.

The End.

I KNOW, I know. I can hardly leave it at that, can I?

After all, it would be impossible to write a book about autism and not include a chapter on you.

My nemesis. My archenemy. My perpetual rival.

People often ask me if I would take autism away if I could.

I'm not sure, to be honest.

Sure, it impacts the way he eats, sleeps, thinks, and learns.

It also adds an exquisite beauty to our world.

Because of autism, I know my neighbor's birthday.

I see the days of the week in color.

When Jack was eight, he walked over to where I was standing at the stove. I was making dinner at the time. Chicken, I think. In his halted tones, he asked me what color I see for Monday.

Autism is okay, is what I am trying to say here. I can work it with it.

You? I would take you away in a heartbeat.

You are fear. You are flight or fight. You are an elevated nervous system in tandem to my own.

Anxiety.

Over the years, I've described you many ways.

You are the snake that winds your away around his spirit, threatening to shorten his breath.

The Cheshire cat smiling around the corner—all wide eyes and silent smirk.

The criminal sitting next to autism in the getaway car, screeching out of the parking lot with all you have stolen from my son—courage and confidence and peace and security.

Anxiety can be difficult to describe. It doesn't fit on a page, or in a conversation.

It should be easy, right?

Let's say your child is scared of the fire drill, or spiders, or the windchill factor.

You soothe him. You smooth his hair and reassure him he is safe.

Anxiety rejects the soothing and smoothing. It is prickly, and annoying, and unlikable.

You manifest in many ways.

Rage, fear, loneliness.

You are the cage that holds him.

And he carries this cage wherever he goes.

Sometimes I think of you as a film.

Not the movie kind of film, with elegant actors and actresses acting out a story, but the Saran wrap kind. You are a thin plastic haze that surrounds him. You blur his features. You drown out his words. You separate us.

At first, I knew nothing about you.

You were a softly whispered word. An impression. A shadow.

You appeared when he was just six years old. You descended upon this earnest first-grader with a vengeance. It was as though the floor dropped right out from beneath him.

All at once, he refused go outside because he was afraid of the cold, even though it was a mild March in New Hampshire.

Then he was afraid to go to the bathroom because one time he went in a public bathroom and the toilet flushed while he was still sitting on it so he could never, ever use one again. He had accidents—lots and lots of 6-year old accidents.

He was terrified of dogs. He worried about them constantly.

He started talking to himself. I don't mean a quiet little reminder to pack pretzels for snack, or a softly hummed nursery rhyme. I mean he was having full-on expressive conversations with himself. He gestured. He grimaced. He jabbed his finger in the air while he muttered.

It chilled me to the bone, watching him converse with an imaginary person inside of his own mind.

We were confused, and perplexed, and scared. One day we had a sunny, albeit quiet and unusual little boy who was working on so many things like how to say *hello* when someone walked in the room and making tons of progress. The next day, he was gone. I don't know how else to describe it.

Hello. Goodbye.

We learned you—all wily fangs and screeching tires—are comorbid to autism. Together, you clasp hands and conspire to steal his joy. No one ever warned us.

Comorbid is an ugly word. It calls to mind darkness and death, which I guess makes sense because even though Jack will never die from your presence, you also don't let him live.

I don't understand your purpose. You have no real value.

Research tells us anxiety is an emotion, often characterized by inner turmoil, dread, and the expectation of a future event.

It is not the same as fear, because fear is the response to a real, actual event.

Science says there are six major types; generalized anxiety disorder, panic attack disorder obsessive-compulsive disorder, phobia, social anxiety disorder, and post-traumatic stress disorder.

The thing is, I don't think you can be reduced to one word, or four syllables, or six disorders.

You eat him from the inside out.

You punch me in the heart. That's what you do.

This is what research and science and Wikipedia and articles don't tell you. They don't explain the way anxiety is a fire that burns around the clock, demanding all the air in the room until my son can hardly breathe.

Medication was our only way out. As much as I hate it, monthly prescriptions are the only way to keep him afloat. Before bed, he shakes a small orange vial into the palm of his hand. Carefully, he washes the pills down with a glass of water.

Still, it isn't a perfect answer. They medicine simply smooths the edges so he can put one foot in front of the other. They don't erase you altogether.

Over the years you've bobbed and weaved your way to the surface again and again.

Teeth lining the shelf on his bed, pulled way too early because the wiggling sensation was too much to bear.

Cuticles bitten raw.

Periods of restless sleep and pre-dawn waking.

Somewhere along the way, you invited your third cousin to the party, completing the slippery trifecta of diagnoses within one boy.

Autism.

Anxiety.

Obsessive Compulsive Disorder.

Now, at nineteen, you lurk behind his eyes. Still, he mutters to himself throughout the day. He keeps to a strict routine. He asks the same question dozens of times a day.

I want to talk to my son.

These are the words I hurl at my husband during yet another debate about the cost of yet another program. My voice is jagged, raw.

I want to talk to my son.

I want a real conversation, beyond what's next on the schedule and what we ate for dinner on Christmas of 2015.

Because of you, he has one foot firmly fixed in the past, and the other rooted in the future. He has no sense of *now* – of living in the moment. He misses so much of what is right in front of him.

His constant questions and need for reassurance feel personal, as though we have no established bond of trust. As ashamed as I am to admit it, I often choose frustration over compassion. I remind myself anxiety is not his fault. It is not a choice.

You are not a choice.

Every day I work to understand you are as much a part of him as his place on the bell curve. You aren't going anywhere. The small white pills keep the snake's hiss at bay. They slow down the getaway car just the tiniest bit. They ease his spirit.

For now.

When it comes to Jack, this is something I say a lot.

For now, he is sleeping.

For now, the pills are working.

For now, there is enough air in the room to breathe.

For now.

I want to talk to my son.

Hello. Goodbye.

15

BE-DO-HAVE

I PLACE my water bottle in the cup holder on the left and slide the safety key toward the right, where it will be out of the way. Bending down, I adjust my laces; first my left foot, then my right. I do it the same way every time. This is my ritual, my tiny ceremony, my transition from ordinary life to this sacred space.

I found my way here thirteen years ago after my youngest son, Henry, was born. At first, it was simply a way to burn off a little baby weight – maybe get forty-five minutes to myself.

The gym I went to at the time had childcare. Every morning, after the bowls and cups from breakfast were loaded in the dishwasher and the crumbs were wiped from the kitchen table, I trundled all five kids out the door. I packed snacks and their favorite DVDs. Using an old alarm clock, I showed Jack how long I would be gone. I made promises of grilled cheese and ice cream afterward.

Once I dropped them off into the big room full of toys and puzzles, I went downstairs to the bank of treadmills lining the walls. In the beginning, I could barely walk for thirty minutes without stopping. I used any excuse to slow down or get a sip of water. Slowly, over the course of six months, I increased my speed and distance.

Miles accumulated became races – a 5K, then a half-marathon. Eventually, I ran the Boston Marathon for the Doug Flutie Foundation.

Sure, I turned to other outlets over the years: yoga, CrossFit, Orangetheory's EPOC workout. Then, a hysterectomy at forty-five paused my endurance. COVID hit six months later, and my workout routine was relegated to a few weights and a rowing machine in the basement. Working out next to the Christmas decorations didn't feel quite the same.

Now, in what is almost a daily religion, I find myself back here again with the cup holder, the safety key, and the laces. The gym is different this time around – one of those 24-hour places that's mostly empty when I go in the morning.

It's been nearly ten years since the alarm clock and DVDs. I come alone. I walk in the door unencumbered. I carry only what I need for myself: a water bottle and headphones.

Treadmill number four.

This is where the work happens.

At first glance, the work seems physical. I sweat. I climb uphill. I push my pace until I am breathless. I stare at the turquoise wall and let my eyes trace over the motivational sayings the gym owner stenciled there.

Don't give up!

Never stop!

You've got this!

I skim the words but rarely examine their meaning. Maybe it's because I've seen them too many times. Mostly, it's because I have my own set of phrases I find more useful.

How you do one thing is how you do everything.

The brain will give up before the body.

It's easier to stay in shape than to get in shape. (This one pushes me forward on the mornings when I'm feeling sluggish and slow – when I am tempted by a second cup of coffee and another scroll through my newsfeed.)

There are days when I hold full-on arguments with Joe and complete conversations with strangers. I write blog posts in my mind. I find deep pockets of courage I didn't know I possessed.

Like a cerebral muscle, I develop my own sense of tenacity. I aim to sprint faster, travel further, and push harder than the day before – all on a machine with black handles and a red stop button.

Ten years later, there is a jaggedness to this routine. At forty-eight, I ponder my own mortality more, perhaps, often than is normal. I am fastidious with appointments and health checks. I never miss a mammogram.

You might say I am trying to delay the inevitable: the day when I'm no longer here for my children, and the most vulnerable one amongst my pack must live without me. It is unthinkable, yet some days, it is all I think about – a constant loop playing inside my brain.

Who will take care of him when I'm gone?

On the treadmill, I catastrophize freely. I visit all my worst-case scenarios with abandon. I go there on purpose.

With my feet moving beneath me, I imagine all the things that could go wrong – Jack could fail spectacularly in this program and come home to live in the basement. Middle school drama, bullying, teenagers getting into car accidents. I don't hold back; I picture it all.

Then, in an attempt at whole-brain thinking, I consider what could go *right*. Henry may navigate eighth grade just fine. Driver's Ed will work its magic and turn bewildered new drivers into experts. Jack will succeed. *He just might succeed.* He might build a life for himself outside of these walls.

With this realization, I am at once flooded with sensations of fear, pride, anxiety, and triumph.

I remind myself of the wisdom someone shared years ago: We don't choose how to feel. Feelings travel to our nervous system faster than language. Judging them is useless and unproductive. As sweat gathers at my temples, I strive to remain curious and open-minded.

Here, I am not just a mother, a wife, a friend, a neighbor.

I am a runner.

Hampered by Imposter's Syndrome, there was a time I could barely utter that sentence out loud. I was afraid people would laugh in my face. How can a middle-aged housewife with five kids possibly consider herself a runner? It sounded like a joke.

At some point, I became fascinated by the power of identity. The way we identify ourselves matters. Identity shapes goals, habits, and behaviors. It creates our inner mantra – the verses of our personal song.

I am a runner. I do what runners do: I buy good sneakers. I follow athletes on social media. I wake up every morning and schedule my time here into my day. I don't let anyone interrupt it.

This concept, also known as *Be-Do-Have*, can apply to almost anything. If you want a garden full of vibrant blossoms and flourishing plants, you must consider yourself a gardener. *Be* a gardener. Then, *do* all the things a gardener would do: read books about planting flowers, buy the right shears and fertilizer, and spend time persuading the earth to grow color. One day, you will look out your window and smile. You *have* a garden.

Today, I'm closer to fifty than forty. You might say I am moving into another season of life, as my kids are beginning to take flight one by one. I am needed less and less. There were years when I longed for the things I have now – freedom, time alone, the ability to come and go as I please. Yet there is a certain hollowness, a yearning to go a few steps backward and do it all differently. Better.

What now?

In many ways, women are made to believe our time is over once our kids are grown. As we head out of our forties, our chances at a new career or project seem to dwindle. We become invisible.

We are fed a narrative that menopausal weight gain is our fate, as the media reduces middle-aged females into a collection of symptoms. Hot flashes. Mood swings. Unattractive dryness.

I don't want this outcome. I want to be sexy. I want to have a swagger in my step and stay fit for as long as possible. Here, with the belt beneath my feet and music in my ears, I feel connected to my younger self again. Despite the crow's feet that bracket my eyes like parentheses or the impending hormonal changes, I am more alive than ever.

With every breath, I dream big. Book proposals, new essays, partnerships. Maybe a job teaching creative writing or working as a ghostwriter. Why not me? Why not now? Anything is possible. Isn't this the very message we tell our kids as we bravely send them off into the world?

My time here is much more than a workout on a machine.

It is my confessional, my racing heart, my breathlessness.

A chance at health, yes, but also a reminder that I'm not finished yet.

Maybe I'm just getting started.

16

THE HEART OF AN ADVOCATE

"IF THIS DOESN'T WORK out, you'll just find another program!"

Your voice was bright – cheerful. You looked at me with an open smile.

It was my second graduation party in as many weeks. I balanced a small white plate in one hand and a napkin in the other, hoping I didn't have any crumbs down the front of my dress.

"Actually," I said, "There really aren't any other programs for him."

"Of course there are!"

"No," I said, "There aren't."

"Well, I'm sure you'll find something."

Standing next to you beneath the evening sky, I felt something wash over me that I could not name.

Anger?

Despair?

Loneliness?

Moments before, we'd been exchanging college stories as we both prepared to launch a child from the proverbial nest.

Your daughter is headed to an Ivy League school. The description of the campus called to mind green leaves folded around brick and old, winding walkways. I offered my congratulations.

Tentatively, I told you about Jack. I mentioned his autism. I explained the residential facility to the full-time staff, the scaffolding, and the teams. You smiled and nodded, but I could tell your mind was beginning to wander a bit.

Where do I begin – in a conversation like this?

At the very start of it all, in a small exam room with the soft-spoken doctor, a whirling toddler, and the three words that changed everything?

Autism Spectrum Disorder.

Or maybe I jump right to the middle . . . when puberty and adolescence wreaked havoc on his 12-year-old spirit.

Standing there, plate in hand, maybe I talk about the fear of self-harm, the way we hid the knives at night, the changes in medication.

Maybe I say that we swore we'd never turn to medication, that we once thought small pills in an orange vial were a sign of weakness or an easy fix. And then, I watched my son descend into anxiety in a way I never witnessed before in my life. Or since.

The air around us was constantly charged with worry. I watched as he lost his smile, his sleep, his potty training, and his joy.

I watched my husband's eyes widen in fear and his voice crack with worry.

How do I tell someone I admire their nonchalance, casualness, and breeziness? How deeply I wish I could stand at a crowded party and suggest there are more programs, more chances, more opportunities?

When it comes to my son and his autism, I can't remember the last time I felt breezy.

Wait. That's not true.

I have a memory that rises to my periphery every once in a while. Two boys side by side in high chairs, wearing matching navy blue pajamas with white snowflakes. Between bites of cheesy pasta, Joe and I answer questions about twins. People admire our growing family.

I looked over at my sons and felt a surge of pride at their likeness, their outstretched palms, their chubby-cheeked health.

October 2004, at an Italian restaurant called Rizzo's. That's the last time I remember not worrying about Jack.

How do you explain the process of obtaining guardianship?

How the State assigned your son his own attorney, you had to hire yours, and you sat at separate tables and watched your 18-year-old's face twist and contort while the lawyers listed all of his vulnerabilities out loud?

How you watched your tall son walk out of the courtroom and reach for his father, and on a rain-soaked morning in early May, you worried you dismantled all you had built?

Maybe I should talk about how there are no other programs for kids like my son Jack.

I could describe the process it took just to find something for him in the first place. The limited programs that can support his needs and simultaneously help him make progress. The *even more limited* spots within the programs.

This might not work.

It might not work even after all it took to get him a spot.

It might not work despite the late-night conversations with my husband – the debates about readiness and maturity.

And if this doesn't work, he will come home.

He will come home to the tune of $80,000 worth of student loans because when it comes to autism, there is no merit money. There are no scholarships. There is no assistance for residential housing with academic scaffolding.

He will come home. And for the rest of our lives, my husband and I will try to fill his days with purpose and meaning. This is what keeps me awake at night.

How do I explain all that, standing in a room full of people and balancing a plate in my hand? It doesn't feel like a cock-tail-party conversation. It feels unfair, to be honest, to dump all of this on you – with your pretty dress and your happy daughter.

How do I capture the complexity that is this boy?

How often do the buzz words "life skills" circle my universe like vultures? Life skills, executive functioning, regulation. A flock of predatory fowls who took up residence in my psyche – all pointy beaks and flying blackness.

Yet, Jack doesn't struggle with life skills.

He can cook a meal. He does his laundry. He wakes up on time and has excellent hygiene.

He manages his medication.

Constantly, I turn this autism balance sheet over in my mind, reducing him to so many checks and balances.

He knows within seconds if someone is sincere. I have no idea how. He can tell if a person wants to talk to him for autism's sake or for *Jack's sake*. There is a difference, you see.

Some want to fake-talk with him so they can go home and sit at the dinner table and exclaim over green beans about how they met a nice boy who had autism, and it was all very good, really.

Others stop what they are doing and hear what he has to offer.

It takes exactly one second for him to tell the difference. If it's the green bean scenario, he just turns around and walks in the other direction. If it's the other way, he begins to share.

It's like watching the ocean meet the shore. The waves lean in close and whisper. They say listen, buddy. I know how many grains of sand you have in your soul.

Do you know what it's like to have an unhappy child? One who perpetually worries about the future while he ruminates about the past?

One who consistently challenges cultural norms?

Who wonders why we say *hello* when we answer the phone, why women wear lipstick, why we shake hands with someone we meet for the first time.

More and more, I'm noticing a push-pull when it comes to autism. It almost resembles a dance – where we nudge him forward, only to draw him back again.

Talk to people.

But don't ask too many questions.

Enjoy the movie/song/show/conversation.

But don't laugh/dance/sing/talk too much.

Learn to feel empathy.

But don't ask about the battle scars.

Always tell the truth.

Unless the truth makes people feel uncomfortable. Then, tell little lies.

There is no such thing as a simple day or an easy explanation.

There is no such thing as normal.

It's easy to assume we all want the same things in life. Friendship, marriage, children. Career, promotion, retirement.

He doesn't want everything I want.

I remind myself it's okay to want different things. It's okay if he's happy with a different life.

After all, a life lived differently is not a life less lived.

Yet, after living alongside autism for seventeen years and watching his heart break, heal, break, heal . . . I forget this central truth.

I want to be better.

I just don't know how.

I am an autism advocate.

Over the years, this has meant many different things. I've changed identities the way one might change a sweater.

At first, Mama Bear. Defensive. Angry. Determined to make everyone see my son for *who* he is rather than *what* he has.

Mama Bear doesn't work. I am very sorry to say this, but it's true. It alienates people. It makes them cling to their original assumptions about autism the way vines cling to a tree.

From there, I became The Apologizer. I apologized to everyone in earshot for the way he jumped, how he grunted, his delay in answering a question.

Slowly, I grew into an advocate. Gently, I told our story. I did this without apology or defense.

I realized I had to be more than an advocate. I had to be a heart-changer – something else entirely.

A heart-changer doesn't just ask for more speech therapy, read articles about gluten-free pretzels, or decide if medication is the right route to take.

A heart-changer stands in front of another person, usually a stranger, and looks inside their mind. You listen carefully to their words and try to figure out what makes them think.

For one single moment, you have to hold their fear, hesitation, and uncertainty in the palm of your hand.

And then, you have to think about your own memories. You have to remember how your father yelled at you, the time you saw a breathtaking butterfly soar through the clouds, and how badly you wanted to grow and be a dancer.

Then, you have to connect the dots, like one of those puzzles you see on the menus in a restaurant.

You say, *oh, you like butterflies? So do I! They remind me of my son Jack.*

There is not a lot of time for the dot-connecting. It might happen in line for the movies, while you are waiting to pick up a pizza, or when buying stamps at the Post Office. You must be quick and open.

As a heart-changer, you have to be willing to celebrate kindness.

You have to be vulnerable.

You have to believe people are good.

I believe people are good. If I don't, I will not be able to live my life. I will exist only inside a bubble of worry and fear and withholding.

I know this: Once in a lifetime, you get to meet a person unlike any other person you have ever met. A person who is complicated, honest, tenacious, and pure.

This person who – well . . . who changes who you thought you were.

And who you planned to become.

He is traveling a lonesome journey of one, yet changing the lives of many.

He is a boy named Jack. He is my child. He is my son.

Sometimes, you can't explain it all, no matter how much time you have. Sometimes, you just need to have faith you planted a tiny seed in someone's preconceived notion of your narrative, and one day, they will look up and see color amidst the black and white.

You hope that one day, she remembers your face and your hope and your child.

Maybe she sees a tall boy and his father walk out of court, and she thinks back to this crowded room and the white plates and the word *autism* hanging in the air.

And she will realize. Things are not always as they seem.

In Italy, they say *Pronto* when they answer the phone. It means ready.

17

FUTURE SELF

LAST WEEK, I took Rose for a routine doctor's appointment. After it was over, we stood in the reception area, making an appointment for next year. Underneath the desk were stacks of paper with the logo *WB Mason* stamped across them.

The late afternoon sun streamed in the windows and landed like a golden pool of light on the W and the B.

And I thought to myself: *One day, I won't be here anymore. But the sun will still shine. WB Mason will keep on making paper. Office managers will order it and stack it by their feet for easy retrieval when the Xerox machine is empty.*

I felt something like deep sadness, more akin to melancholy than tears.

I mean, it's not as though I don't consider my own mortality. Of course, I do. Every special-needs mother worries about leaving a vulnerable child behind.

I am desperate to know how this story ends. Only you can answer that.

Yet you are not real – yet. You are an ethereal version of my same-day self.

I have so many questions.

Did anyone buy this book? How did the cover come out?

I planned to use a photo of Jack. The one we took in Italy when we visited the town where Joe's mother was born. It was raining that day. Walking through the cobblestone streets, we told Jack to put the umbrella over his head.

Taken from behind, the image captures him perfectly in my mind: his literalness, his determination, his courage in the rain.

Sometimes, I try to picture you.

White hair? A deeply lined face?

Hunched over a walker or standing straight and tall?

How old are you? How far did we make it? Seventy? Eighty?

Is it a tumor? Cancer?

Dementia? Alzheimer's?

Something I love to do is catastrophize. I imagine the very worst-case scenario. Teenagers smashed up in cars, every twinge a disease. A forgotten actor's name is the gateway to me wandering down the road without my shoes – or worse, my shirt.

There is no middle ground here. No fender benders or stomach bug for me, no sir! If I don't remember Matthew McConaughey was in The Wedding Planner, I am doomed! Also, it just took me three tries to spell McConaughey, so clearly, the decline has started in the cognitive department.

As I see it, a catastrophizer isn't the same as, say, a hypochondriac. We don't limit ourselves to the physical domains of our body. We *extend*, if you will.

Last year, a tragedy shook our town to its very core. Seeing a mother's grief up close is a little like touching the surface of the sun. It is searing with rawness. It made me adjust my own priorities a little.

This is what disaster does. It shakes our brains like a snow globe and forces us to recognize how stupid we are to long for anything more than the basics. Health. Safety. The same number of faces around the dinner table we started with in the morning.

It's like updating the prescription to an old pair of glasses. What was once plain becomes sublime – the ordinary is magnificent. We hold it all in the palm of our hand.

Still, it's not perfect. I yell about dumb things, like the time Charlie backed over a bike in the garage when he was learning to drive – or how Henry takes forever to get out the door in the morning. Joey eating my leftovers because, to my oldest, *what's mine is his*.

Yet I am trying new things, new tactics. When I veer toward irritability and frustration, I close my eyes and practice my 5-5-5 rule. It's a little something I came up with during the Charlie-and-the-bike scenario.

Will this matter in five minutes? Five days? Five years.

No. No. No.

Rarely does it matter past five minutes. And when it does . . . well, I pay attention.

I'm working hard to pull back from the teenagers – to stop hovering and nagging. My new thing is when I think they are in over their head with classes or the baseball schedule or Driver's Ed, I don't launch into lectures about time management and organization.

Instead, I ask.

I ask how I can help them be most successful.

Their answers are usually simple. Can I pick up index cards at the store or wash a dirty uniform? Can we have meatloaf for dinner?

Perhaps the hardest part of having teenagers is you can't fix their problems. They have to figure it out themselves. The most annoying truth is that the answer they arrive at on their own is the one that really sticks.

Do we ever talk, Jack and I?

I mean, of course, we talk. We talk all the time. Some might even say too much.

Yet it is an exchange of information, the same way court reporters trade facts.

We talk about the weather. Celebrities. Anything pop culture or recipes involving Oreos.

It's not a conversation.

I want to talk to my son.

This is what I screamed at Joe, all hoarse voice and hysteria, after a particularly fraught argument about the cost of college programs.

I want to talk to my son.

I want to know how he feels about politics, the environment . . .

I want to know if he dreams in color or if his nighttime musings are as black and white as his daytime thoughts.

Does he live on his own? That is the million-dollar question. It's what we're all perched on the edge of our seats to know.

Does he have a roommate? Or a companion? Does he fall in love?

Neuroscience tells us our brains to arrive at a conclusion; then, it looks for evidence to support it.

For as long as I can remember, I was committed to one outcome: Jack would need me forever. Then, I scoured for clues.

I focused on his vulnerabilities—how he struggles to sign his name, how he thinks cars cost $500, and his difficulty connecting with peers. In some ways, without meaning to, I kept him young.

See, there is this duality in Jack. His physical age and his emotional age. Physically, his body is that of a young man. Yet emotionally, he lags behind by about six years.

Constantly, I focused on the younger version. Now, I'm trying to bridge the gap by acknowledging them both.

He might not need me forever.

This is good and right. It is scary and sad. It is change. It is a new outcome.

I'm working on the catastrophizing part. Instead of imagining all that could go wrong, I try to think of what might go right.

Instead of smashed-up car wrecks, teenagers might enjoy a fun night out with friends. Maybe they'll eat tacos with lots of sour cream. Crowded into tiny booths, they'll glance at one another and smile.

Instead of cancer, maybe it's nothing more than a pulled muscle.

Instead of stumbling without me, he may actually learn to fly on his own.

The word *instead* is important here. It's where our brain switches gears and moves from fear to possibility.

I call this my *whole-heart thinking*.

Anyway, that's where I'm at right now.

It might be the best it gets. Who can say?

What I really want to know is: *How is life for you, future me?*

Are you happy? Do your knees work? I'm trying very hard to keep the knees moving and not stressing them out too much. If you're anything like me now, we need to run a lot.

What about Joe?

Joe. A face I know better than my own. Please tell me he is still holding my hand. Tell me he's here. Because the truth is, I cannot bear life without him.

We have found an ease I never imagined. We have found space and time that doesn't feel stolen. In this easy-ish season of marriage. I wish we could take back all that was once wrong between us—the pettiness, the meanness, the arguments.

Did you ever stop hating yourself? Not full-blown hate, but the teeny seeds of self-loathing that sometimes wake you in the night. Do they ever go away?

What about Jack?

This question is the vibration of my day—the perpetual loop inside my mind.

Where does he live? Does he have a job? Does he ever stop swearing? Is he alone? Is he lonely?

I am terrified he will spend his life alone.

Tomorrow, we drop him off at his new program.

I know you think you didn't do enough.

Memories of Henry and Boston weigh heavily in your heart.

A pink girl stretched out on the bed, her heart full of worry.

All the times you yelled and criticized.

I hope you remember the times you stayed up late, listening to their chatter, their problems, their laughter, their sadness.

The trips to the beach with ice cream afterward, the library books found beneath beds, the last-minute Halloween costume when Henry decided he wanted to be a gangster.

There are things in life that cannot be bought or owned. A teenager's smile, waves on the shore, forgiveness.

Forgive yourself.

You did enough.

We did our best.

You gave them all you had.

Tomorrow, I will let go of all that is meaningful in the shape of a boy.

How does it turn out?

Who am I now, in your time and space?

The truth is that office managers will order paper. Late afternoon sun will slant through the blinds. Perhaps this is the very essence of mortality – the ache you feel when you see the golden orange light, knowing you won't be here to witness the brilliance. No one will care. They will simply continue to make appointments and feed the printer.

I don't know what the future holds. I guess I'll make my own version. My own little time-hop, if you will. Even if it doesn't come true, it sure beats imagining tumors wrapped around my insides or a brain gone spongy like a soft-boiled egg.

Thirty years from now. That seems like a good place. Two years shy of eighty.

Joe and I sit on the front porch. It's summertime. We're waiting for people, waiting to start a celebration of some kind. A barbecue, a birthday party, an ice cream cake waiting in the freezer.

I look over at this man. His hair is almost entirely white – like his father's was at this age. It makes for a beautiful contrast to the chocolate brown eyes that have met my gaze for so long.

One by one, our kids trickle home. Except they aren't kids anymore. They are full-grown people. They jump out of cars and minivans. They unbuckle car seats and unload sullen teenagers. Joe and I meet them on the walkway. We kiss cheeks, admire outfits, and take babies upon our hips.

This beautiful jumble of mismatched people belongs to me, bound as we are by a silvery familial thread.

Mine, yet not mine, for our children never really belong to us in the first place, do they?

I am breathless with long runs, good jokes, and funny stories. I am breathless with life.

After a moment, another car pulls up the long driveway. Self-driving, it turns off on its own. A tall man steps out from the driver's side. He is silhouetted against the summer sky. At nearly fifty, silver threads his once-dark hair. In the curve of his face, I recognize every version he once was.

Mischievous toddler.

Restless teenager.

Young man.

A shadow moves in the passenger seat. The door opens. Collectively, our gaze shifts.

"Mom. Dad. I'd like you to meet my friend."

18

DEAR JACK

YOU AND I stand together in the kitchen. We've done this thousands of times before.

You've always been my early-morning riser. For eighteen years, I've listened for you as the purple dawn met the sunrise.

Fussy infant.

Mischievous toddler.

Restless teenager.

We've stood in this same spot – me with my coffee, you with a box of waffles in your hands – yet this morning feels different.

It is our last tender meeting in the early yellow light.

Carefully, you put waffles into the toaster. You cross the room to get the syrup from the cabinet.

You flick your fingers together lightly – a familiar sign of excitement and adrenaline.

We don't talk much; we never have. We simply orbit each other. To the casual observer, it is almost a choreographed dance as I make my way to the coffee pot for a refill while you pass me silently to reach into the drawer for a fork.

It's July. A month smack-dab in the middle of summer with humid air and empty sky. For weeks, New Hampshire has endured a spell of dry weather. The grass in the backyard is dry and brittle from the lack of rain.

For weeks, you've been organizing and re-organizing – the pots and pans for the kitchen you'll share, the popcorn maker, the pancake griddle. You folded your clothes neatly into the trunk from graduation.

The last few days, we took a farewell tour to all your treasured spots: lunch at the local cafe for your favorite chicken fingers and a chat with your beloved server, a drive by the park where you first learned to kick your legs and swing, the elementary school with the tennis courts.

The car is packed. Your new comforter – carefully chosen at Bed, Bath, and Beyond – blue with white stripes. A duffel bag full of school supplies.

Once there, we will unpack it.

We'll carefully unload all that is meaningful to you.

I'll make your bed like I've done thousands of times before. I'll smooth the sheets over the mattress pad and slide pillow into pillowcase. We'll stack the new towels in the bathroom. We'll arrange your new shirts in the drawer.

There is a barbecue lunch.

Over burgers and salad, we'll meet the people who will take this autism journey from here – the baton carriers of life skills, academic support, and residential life.

We'll meet your roommates. We'll make tentative small talk with other parents and exchange nervous smiles.

When it is time to go, I imagine we'll all troop back outside into the sun's glare – a family of seven about to contract and shrink by one.

At some point, you will walk one way.

And we will walk the other.

Beneath a jealous summer sky, we will separate.

It will be perhaps the hardest moment of my life.

People ask if I am ready.

The truth is, a mother is never ready.

She is never ready to alter the familial landscape upon which she has built her life.

Yet, I know it is *time*.

See, my son, readiness and time rarely share the same clock.

I built my world around you. I didn't choose this. It is simply life alongside a diagnosed child.

Appointments, speech therapy, meetings, paperwork.

Weekend hours spent filling your time as a means of productivity combined with – fingers crossed! – skill building.

Errands to the pharmacy to demonstrate prescription-filling. The bank for deposits – your name carefully signed on the bottom of the slip. The local sandwich place for lunch, with prompts for eye contact and using your napkin.

Round and round we went, circling our small town until we wore our smooth tracks in winding back roads and shopping plazas.

Autism connected us together in the complicated ways.

For eighteen years, we were a "we."

I spoke when you couldn't find the words.

My regulation was the barometer for your own.

I fought. I sat in stuffy conference rooms and made a case for inclusion and behavior therapy. I wrote emails. I made phone calls.

When a doctor tried to capture your language delay by telling us to imagine everyone is speaking French but you, I imagined unfamiliar vowels and consonants circling wildly in your mind.

Through it all, I rooted for you.

I rooted for you, and although I couldn't quite picture it, somewhere in my deep subconscious, I hoped for this day.

Jack, so often I worried we would lose you to the inner world of autism – to the long beckoning finger of isolation, obsessiveness, and anxiety.

I'll never forget the night when you were eight, and we all watched The Wizard of Oz together.

At the end of the movie, you sat up straight and announced, "The Lion. He has autism."

I asked you why? Why did you think that?

"Because he is afraid. All the time."

My Jack-a-boo. Only then did I understand the perpetual fear which lives within your heart.

Yet now, on this morning, I keep thinking how brave you are.

To leave behind all that is good and familiar – in hopes that the unknown may offer something better.

In many ways, this is the end of your childhood.

I used to joke that the umbilical cord once connecting us has merely stretched over time. It never fully severed. You and I have always been bound together – our nervous systems intertwined like kite strings.

Wherever I am, you are – reciting the latest movie review, reminding me we're low on paper towels, musing about the number of spiders found in Brazil.

Your first word was ball.

Mom wasn't second or even third.

Now, it is the tympani of my background – the perpetual vibration throughout my day.

Mom.

For Mom. I am home.

But Mom. We need to buy eggs.

I wish people could see how far you've come.

How, once upon a time, you were crushed by an indelible anxiety.

How you raged and suffered through puberty and early adolescence.

The way you held my hand in the parking lot, and you couldn't sit through your brother's basketball game without shrieking, and how chicken fingers were all you wanted for dinner.

Yet beneath it all you had a quiet resilience and a tender spirit. We chose to focus on that. We decided to develop *who you are* instead of who we thought you should be.

See, Jack-a-boo, raising children is a little like growing wildflowers.

Some need more water than others. Some need extra fertilizer or a certain kind of soil. Some tilt their silky blossoms to the bright orange sun and soak in as much heat as possible, while others curl inward toward the cool, dark shade.

But in time, they all bloom. They all open their petals and offer their brilliant color to the world.

I guess what I'm saying is it's not about where you go but how you got there in the first place.

From the time you were little, we did the hard things. We put you back in your chair seventeen-thousand-five hundred times so you would know how to sit through dinner, use your napkin, and eat with a fork.

We insisted you wear a shirt – even when you were in your no-shirt phase.

We chased you through the mall so you would learn to hold our hands.

We played a game that we named after those brightly colored plastic bricks to show you how to climb steps one leg at a time: *one Lego, two Lego, three Lego.*

We taught you how to stay seated until the bus stopped, and we helped you figure out how to tie sneakers with laces so you wouldn't be the only boy in school still wearing Velcro.

We showed you how to pray.

I pushed, I told social stories, I redirected, I reminded.

You know what else I did?

I let perfect be the enemy of good.

I should have inhaled your sweet-smelling hair after a bath.

I should have been more patient when you wanted to watch another Baby Einstein video.

I should have put down the laundry basket, sat on the carpet, and stacked blocks with you.

I should have made life wait.

I should have made autism wait.

Don't mind me, Jack-a-boo, as I reach my fingers toward the hot flame of regret.

We were not perfect. It's true.

But I did the very best I could.

We did the work, yet still, I feel like there is an hourglass bolted down on our kitchen counter, and we only have so long until the sand filters to the bottom.

Was it enough? Is it enough? Will it be enough?

You probably don't remember this, Jack-a-boo, but when you were about three, I wore a necklace with the word *believe* spelled on it.

It wasn't expensive. I bought it at the salon where I got my hair cut after a particularly bad week.

I wore it every day. And when you started to descend into another meltdown at the store or scream in the early hours of dawn, I'd show it to you and whisper softly *I believe in you, Jack. I believe in you. I believe in you.* Somehow, in some way, it centered us both.

I hope one day you look back on this time fondly. I hope you remember there were more good days than bad – more laughter than tears. I hope it was more than social stories, occupational therapy, speech, and autism.

After all, how do you measure childhood?

How do you measure thousands of moments strung together like brightly colored beads on a string?

Sandcastles, jellybeans, snowstorms, stomach bugs, faded beach towels, pillow forts, milk for Santa.

Burnt cookies, arguments over hats in winter, bikes left out in the rain.

Lullabies, and quick goodbyes, and smiles off the bus.

Messy conversations, late-night confessions.

Heartache, heartbreak, heartbeat.

Every time I look at you, I see your toddler face, your newborn gaze, your sixth-grade grin.

I am reminded of your Mother's Day arrival on a springtime Sunday morning. You arrived in a fury – determined from the onset to make your own way.

It will be an adjustment for all of us. The days ahead are both bitter and sweet.

And in your darkest moments – when you are homesick or overwhelmed or anxious – remember.

You are not alone.

Behind you stands a family.

A family full of inside jokes and funny memories and sad times and mostly good stuff.

One girl, three brothers, and a devoted father.

We were so tempted to keep you here, in this house, in this town, in this life.

Like a bird in a gilded cage, we longed to protect you. We weren't sure you were ready to fly. We didn't know how to let you go.

I didn't think about it. That's the truth. Until this quiet morning meeting, I didn't let myself consider living in this house without you.

Instead, I slogged through March's gray days. I watched you pull out the Easter decorations – the tall glass jar for jellybeans, rabbits, and plastic eggs – and I shielded my eyes from the imminent summer sun.

At the very same time, I lived inside the realm of the coming year.

I saw the green pancake batter you mixed so carefully the night before St. Patrick's Day, and hot tears pricked my eyelids.

I leaned against the refrigerator door and wondered *who I am without you.*

In the early light this morning, I see your gaze shift around the kitchen. I watch you hold the dog close and stroke his soft fur.

And I wonder *who you are without us.*

You see, autism is a riddle of contradictions.

It is a push-pull not unlike the ocean's tide or how the evening sun draws toward dusk.

I wanted this so badly for you. Yet now that it's upon us, I'm unsure how to let you go.

You seem excited. You talk about meeting your roommate and how you can walk to the grocery store and maybe take a class in broadcasting.

But it's hard to know how much you understand all that will change for you.

I pushed for this; can you see that?

I pushed for it because I was convinced you could do it.

I pushed for it because I wanted more for you.

But what if it's too much?

What if someone hurts you, preys on you, steals your money, hits you in the crosswalk, bullies you?

It will be my fault.

This is my truth.

Autism changed me. Yes, it made me curious, aware, and accepting,

It also made me suspicious.

We've taught you how to change a lightbulb, hang Christmas lights, shake hands, order a cheeseburger, call your grandparents, fold towels, pick out gifts, and answer the front door.

I don't know how to teach you how to be to be wary – watchful.

This is why I tell our story, Jack.

I have to tell about autism and the work and the fear and the worry.

I have to share our small triumphs, moments of light, gentle intentions, radical grace, reckless mercy, and tender, tender resilience.

Because if compassion is a house we build, then storytelling is the key to the front door.

It is the entrance to our messy kitchens and our lopsided picture frames and our wildly unguarded hearts.

It is the only way to throw open the windows and bring in the sun.

I don't know what the future holds. I don't know if you can sit through a college class, learn to budget money, or lease an apartment on your own.

So, we'll do what we always do. We'll try.

After all, a wave returns over and over again to kiss the shore, no matter how many times it's turned away.

It is time to make some new tracks.

It is easy to assume our story is a story about an autism diagnosis when, in fact, it is much, much more.

It is the story of a tender father coming to terms with the foreverness that is raising a complicated child – a child who may never earn for himself, understand a mortgage, or raise a family of his own.

It is the story of a world so seemingly narrow . . . that there is no choice but to pull it apart cloud by cloud.

It is a story of a family's return to the basics: dinner at the table every night, Sunday mornings at Grandma's, and ice cream on hot summer days.

In the now.

This is where I work to stay.

Desperately, frantically, I try to keep my brain in the present space rather than spiraling backward into the dark pool of regret or leapfrogging forward to a future that is hazy at best.

Every once in a while, I fast-forward to different versions of you.

You at forty, sixty-three, seventy-five.

I can't quite see them. My mind's eye draws a blank white space.

Who will order your birthday cake?

Who will you eat Christmas dinner with – or Easter Brunch?

It is this very white space that propels me forward.

I must push you into the world, even as I long to keep you from it.

I must disentangle myself from your story, even as I long to stay a main character. It is the only way to help you build a life full of richness and color.

You are ready, even as I am not.

At the same time, I wish I could have it all back again.

The nights around the television watching the Tin Man, green pancakes on a white plate, a staircase made of Legos.

With all my heart, I want it back. Yet I know it is time for you to try to fly.

I believe in you. I always have.

My wizard. My lion. My heart full of hope.

My wild child, my game-changer, my Sunday son.

You are true and whole and right and good.

And in your own way, in your own time, I know you will set the world alight.

My little boy.

Reach for the sky.

I can't wait to see what you do with this one and only life you call yours.

I still look for you every time I pull into the garage.

I only know a single phrase in French.

Je t'aime.

Je t'aime, my Jack-a-boo.

I love you.

EPILOGUE

FROM THE TREES, I watch. A red minivan pulls into the parking lot. The building is brick. It stands three stories high. It gives the impression of age with a fresh coat of paint.

A man, a woman. Four boys and a girl. One by one, they step out; without a word, they gather. They look toward the door and back at each other.

This is a family. You can tell by the resemblance – their height, mannerisms, and shared smiles.

There is a vulnerable one amongst them. A boy they have learned to watch for, speak for, and protect.

The tallest hops lightly. He rubs his hands together and adjusts his glasses. He is excited. He is ready.

He has been waiting for this day. A fire has been lit. Once you make flame from air, you cannot extinguish it. Everyone knows this. The air is too charged. It is electric.

The father opens the trunk. They each step forward and begin to unload. One boy seems to be the oldest. He wears glasses.

He is very strong. He takes a box full of stuff for a kitchen – spatulas and dishes and silverware – and walks inside, all squared shoulders and deliberate stride.

The smallest boy, perhaps twelve or thirteen, races ahead with a box in his hands. He wants to be the first to see the building.

They dodge puddles left by the rainstorm that briefly interrupted the summer sun. Though their feet dance around the small pools of water, there is a heaviness to their steps and their hearts.

The mother pauses. She looks to the sky. She thinks of blue. She thinks of sandcastles. She thinks of newborns swaddled in snug blankets.

The dark-haired boy grabs the big trunk full of T-shirts and bath towels. He moves quickly. He smiles at people waiting by the door with their name tags.

The girl watches the tallest. She feels his energy as though it is her own. Skeptically, she appraises the people with the name tags; when it comes to her big brother, she has learned to trust no one.

In and out they go, working quickly. Within about twenty minutes, the job is finished. The car is empty. Meanwhile, other cars have parked, and a similar tableau ensues. Families encircle their vulnerable own. Trunks are emptied. Puddles are dodged.

After an hour or so, they all disappear – bees into the proverbial hive.

From my perch, I imagine beds made. Spatulas set into drawers. T-shirts folded and re-folded.

Soon, a large grill is lit. People gather again outside. They make plates of food. They talk, but they don't say what they mean.

They exchange stories about summer trips and the best local beach spots. They praise the meal – burgers hot off the grill, salad with fresh tomatoes.

This mother nods politely at everyone, but her mind is stuck on her son. She watches him out of the corner of her eye. She resists the urge to remind him to use his napkin. She considers the question he asked earlier that morning as they stood together in the tangerine light.

No one speaks the words hovering around their periphery.

What if this doesn't work?

What if this is the last stop?

What other options are available for the diagnosed, the quirky, the neurodiverse? The road to this parking lot was long. It was full of obstacles. It comes with a hefty price tag.

Every story needs an enemy. An antagonist.

Who is the enemy here?

Autism?

That doesn't feel quite right.

Maybe anxiety . . . and the way it loops and binds his soul – tethering him to unnamable fear.

It is one story, but it is everyone's story. A story of overcoming and becoming.

Soon, it is time to leave. The family finds themselves alone in the parking lot once again. They circle him – like petals around the heart of a flower. Mother-father-brother-brother-sister-brother.

The father squints off into the distance. He thinks of fire escapes, online predators, bullies, and mean people.

One by one, they give him quick hugs.

The tall boy turns. He walks away. He crosses the pavement and opens the door.

The dark-haired boy calls out a final farewell. The youngest shades his eyes. He blinks.

The mother is a container. She holds it all inside. She watches her husband and oldest son embrace. They lean against one another and wipe the tears away.

The girl stands off to the side, alone. She is pink beneath the sunshine. Inside each sob is a story all her own. A tale of mice, of men, of empty seats on the bus, and years of flying through the mines in search of yellow, of feathers, of a battle cry in her brother's name.

We are meant to remember some days forever.

Dear family.

Let him find his life.

He will find his life.

Like a bird on a tree, he will take unsteady, extraordinary flight.

As they drive away, she thinks of his question.

For Mom. Did you ever think this day would come?

ACKNOWLEDGMENTS

My deepest gratitude to those who held my words in the palm of their hands and saw the book before it was whole.

To each and every follower who found a piece of themselves inside our story. Who rooted for us on the days we couldn't even root for ourselves.

For Melissa, who gave me space to learn how to write.

For Kate and Adrian, who took me under their virtual wing.

For Jessica Daniels, who encouraged me to make the leap into self-publishing.

Sarah Mayor, who patiently coaxed edits in the final hour.

Christopher Vazquez, for tirelessly working to help this book reach far and wide.

Lyn Silarski, for working magic with the design.

Audrey, Maureen, and Barbara, for friendship, support, and laughter.

Chastity and Elaine, my touchstones and sounding board.

Joseph, my oldest son. Our fearless leader.

Charlie, the middle child, the boy with the chocolate eyes. May the stars always shine.

My daughter, Rose. You are perfect as you are.

My youngest, Henry. The boy I nearly lost. And then I found.

My husband, Joe. It is your voice I hear as I type.

And Jack, Jack-attack, Jack-a-boo. Watching you take flight is breathtaking.

ABOUT THE AUTHOR

Carrie Cariello lives in Southern New Hampshire with her husband, Joe, their five teenagers, and their beloved dog, Wolfie.

She is the author of <u>What Color Is Monday, How Autism Changed One Family for the Better</u>, and <u>Someone I'm With Has Autism</u>.

Carrie is a regular contributor to the Huffington Post, TODAY Parents, the TODAY Show, Parents.com, Love What Matters, and Grown and Flown. She has been interviewed by NBC Nightly News and has a <u>TEDx talk</u>.

She speaks regularly about autism, marriage, and motherhood, and writes a weekly blog at <u>www.carriecariello.com</u>. One of her essays, <u>"I Know What Causes Autism,"</u> was featured as one of the Huffington Post's best of 2015, and her piece, <u>"I Know Why He Has Autism,"</u> was named one of the top blog posts of 2017 by the TODAY Show.

Carrie grew up in a tiny town in rural New York. It had one stop light. Back then she was Carrie Watterson, and she was always the tallest girl in her class.

After high school, Carrie got a Bachelor of Science in Political Administration from the State University of New York and a Masters in Public Administration from Rockefeller College. During this time, she met a dark-haired guy named Joe. He dreamed of becoming a dentist. On Easter Sunday in 1996, in her little apartment above a hair salon, he gave her a small sapphire ring. They laughed and cried and planned a wedding.

Together they moved to Buffalo, New York, where he went to dental school and Carrie began a career in marketing.

While they were in Buffalo they had a son, Joseph. About a year later, they had another son, Jack.

From the time he was a small baby wearing dark blue pajamas with snowflakes, Jack was different. He did not talk, babble or coo. He did not point. He did not have things like joint attention or gross motor skills or eye contact.

What he did have, Joe and Carrie eventually learned, was autism.

They went on to have another boy and they named him Charlie. After Charlie was born in 2005 they moved to Bedford, New Hampshire.

Carrie did not dream of becoming a writer as a little girl in rural New York. She did not have visions of tap-tap-tapping her life story on a laptop for people to read on Facebook or in a blog or a book. But over time, she learned she could best make sense of her long, frustrating days with Jack and his autism if she wrote about them. Over time, writing helped her separate the boy from his diagnosis. She discovered that she fiercely loves them both.

Like a prism with countless different angles and light, sometimes she sees her own reflection in her words. Sometimes she understands herself better.

Every day, she makes herself move forward to post, to publish, to reveal. People seem to like it. People are following her. Like the prism, people see tiny colorful bits of themselves and their families and their children in her essays.

She and the dark-haired guy from college have been married for twenty-five years, and together they have four boys and one rosy daughter. Some days are long and difficult and exhausting, while others are filled with color and music and chocolate-covered doughnuts. They are filled with laughter and love.

ALSO BY CARRIE CARIELLO

What Color Is Monday,

How Autism Changed One Family for the Better

Excerpt

Making Progress: Stretch, Don't Break

With a child who has been evaluated, tested, and analyzed as much as Jack has, the real challenge comes after all the reporting and results: the real challenge is translating those test results into practical applications which will help him make progress.

In our early days of autism, back when Jack was a chubby, blue-eyed toddler, much of our daily lives revolved around encouraging his language and keeping him engaged. When he was about a year old we started using sign language for simple commands like "more" and "all done".

When he was just under two, we made pictures of his favorite food and toys. We posted them all over the house so he could point to what he wanted instead of screaming. One of Joe's fondest memories is of Jack walking to the refrigerator, pointing to a picture of Cheerios in a snack cup, and pretending to eat them. It was a Cheerio breakthrough; he was identifying the food and engaging in pretend play.

Once he did start speaking consistently around age three, we constantly encouraged him to use his words. I distinctly remember tapping my lips with my forefinger over and over, asking him to "Say it. *Say* cookie, Jack. Say it." A behavioral therapist warned us to be careful about anticipating his needs; instead we should give him the chance to articulate what he wanted, even if it meant building time into our routine to accommodate his pace. She suggested giving him choices throughout the day so he could exercise and grow his vocabulary.

Say it.

In addition to language, we were always trying to get him to look us in the eye. Another popular line in our growing repertoire of commands was "Look at me". Whenever I spoke to him, I would kneel down to his level and place my fingers on his chin to connect his gaze with mine. We named things for him incessantly, pointing with an exaggerated gesture to direct his attention.

Mama. Dada. Cup. Bird.

After a while, every interaction with little Jack began to feel deliberate, orchestrated towards some faraway goal. I complained one day to our speech therapist that nothing felt spontaneous with him, every one of his actions had a reaction, and every nuance of his behavior was recorded and examined. "It will", she soothed. "You'll see how much easier this will get."

Sometimes it didn't feel worth it. It didn't feel like repeating "Look in my eyes" a hundred times a day could possibly release this little boy from his inner sanctum or that sign language would lead to actual words out of his precious mouth. Sometimes I just wanted to let him watch those Baby Einstein movies he loved so much; to be and let be.

And sometimes I did.

But for the most part, we were consistent in our efforts to draw him out and pull him towards us. We stretched ourselves. And little by little, it paid off; like a baby bird cracking out of his shell, Jack slowly broke through his silence and began to chirp. He'd always been very affectionate and physical, but his affections became more directed and focused. It felt as though he'd joined our family at last.

Officially diagnosed with PDD-NOS in 2005, we'd held off on any psychological testing until the fall of 2011. Every year he was evaluated for his academic Individual Education Plan (IEP), and we met with a developmental pediatrician off and on in both Buffalo and New Hampshire. When he was in seven and in the second grade we started to really wonder more about how Jack's brain works; how he learns and processes. Now that he could communicate more effectively, we'd begun to notice he really does see the world very differently, and perhaps we would have more success tapping into that fascinating mind if we understood it better.

Once presented with the test results, I started to panic. How could we ever take all of this information and package it so we had a plan of attack? His issues seemed so widespread; could we really teach Jack to move the sound of a siren to the back of his brain and concentrate on his spelling instead? How do you increase a person's theory of mind? We'd moved from reminding him to make eye contact and notice a squirrel outside the window to trying to teach him that he can handle the sensation of a loose tooth.

I was overwhelmed.

So, with the help of our psychologist, we took the lengthy report bullet by bullet, problem by problem, and created a strategy to address each of Jack's challenges. We aren't going to solve Jack's autism all at once - the idea is to increase his ability in each of the identified areas; self-regulation, communication, and cognitive ability. Essentially, we want Jack to learn to stretch himself like a rubber band, but have the skills to identify his breaking point before he snaps.

Regulation

This winter I enrolled the boys in ski and snowboarding lessons every Monday, and after an hour of snowboarding one thing was clear; Jack's body felt good. On the car ride home he was present, engaged, and peaceful. He joked and laughed with his brothers; one week he even developed a game and explained it to them. I began to notice the correlation between his level of physical activity and his ability to participate in the world around him.

Jack adapts to his surroundings and learns best when his body feels ready, when the ants of self-stimulation are quiet and his mind is calm. Exercise and movement are essential for him to feel regulated.

Now, if we notice he has the "zoomies" and needs to stim, we direct him towards the mini-trampoline in the playroom or his bike outside. If the weather's good, we try to squeeze in a few scooter rides down our long driveway before school in the morning. At school they have him perform things like wall push-ups and jumping jacks if he seems deregulated.

Our psychologist advised that the trick is to get Jack to notice his body's arousal *before* it hits what we sometimes call the "red zone"; where he's past the point of no return, like the evening of the holiday light show. She suggested using a program call "How Does Your Engine Run". At school Jack made a small booklet identifying how his body feels, and what the appropriate activity would be in response. It's attached to a keychain and he keeps it with him throughout the day.

I try to ask him how his engine feels a few times a day and get him to label the sensation of his body. One time he was in a rage because I told him he'd had enough marshmallows for the day, and then I added insult to injury by asking him in that exact moment how his body felt. "Mad and hungry!" I asked him what he could do about that, hoping he would solve his own problem and suggest jumping on the trampoline. Nope.

"Eat another marshmallow!"

Another time he was snuggled up in front of the fireplace watching one of his beloved Baby Einstein videos, surrounded by assorted stuffed animals and brothers. His face looked relaxed and his body was limp. I asked him how his engine felt.

"Just right."

As important as it is for Jack to stay calm, it's just as important for the adults in his world to remain composed. When he gets aroused, it's very tempting for me to mirror his distress, raise my voice, and meet him in the red zone. Now I force myself to keep it together, and sometimes I even repeat "just right" to myself - my job is to get him to feel "just right".

Communication

Jack's communication issues are twofold; he struggles with both expressing himself and receiving complex verbal information. Each of these are further compromised when he's in a stressful situation or deregulated.

I wish there was an easy answer or fix for his communication problems, that something as concrete as jumping on a trampoline or covering up a work sheet could produce tangible results. Instead, Joe and I have incorporated our psychologist's concept "low and slow" into our parenting approach.

Low and slow means pretty much what it says; keep your voice low and your words slow. This was not an intuitive way for me to communicate with my kids - I prefer the "high and fast method" myself. It's taken a fair amount of practice for me to slow down and lower my voice when I'm agitated. All of us are slowly stretching.

Luckily, our larger family gives Jack a lot of opportunity to spontaneously interact. Unaware of his specific communication problems, his siblings expect answers when they ask Jack a question, and all but demand his participation in their play. Six-year old Charlie is especially adept at drawing Jack out; "Jack, I asked you if you want milk or juice. Milk or *juice*?"

I do have to remind the kids to keep it low and slow for Jack, to give him time to listen and respond. Basically we all have to accept his limitations and give him room to stretch and grow.

In school Jack receives speech therapy twice a week. At this point they're focusing on improving his conversation skills and social communication. Also, one day a week he selects a friend to join him back in the classroom for "lunch bunch", a time for them to enjoy a quiet meal together and work on his peer interaction.

And for those moments when Jack's in the red zone and simply can't find the words, we've created visual tools to aid him. At school he has a thermometer where he drew different temperature zones to indicate how he feels in a heated moment. Helping him label his internal temperature will hopefully lead to greater emotional competence and increase his ability to tolerate certain feelings for longer periods of time.

Cognitive Flexibility & Theory of Mind

A few months ago I was proudly telling our psychologist about how Jack had been making breakfast for Joey before school each morning. To my delight, sometimes I came downstairs and found two identical bowls of cereal and cups of juice arranged at the counter.

I was pleased with both his initiative and independence, but she gently reminded me that it's also a sign of his limited theory of mind: he assumed Joey wanted the same meal he did. (Luckily, Joey is pretty flexible.) In an effort to stretch his cognitive ability, she suggested we have him *ask* his brother what he'd like to eat. Now we have a game we play called "Waiter", where he takes a pen and paper and asks everyone in the house what they're in the mood for. (Note: This can backfire. Charlie asked for shrimp lo mein for lunch last week. He got peanut butter and jelly instead.)

We try and work in small cognitive exercises like this throughout our day to encourage Jack to notice how the people around him might think or feel. One night his older brother was ticked off because we'd told him to shut the Wii off and go to bed. As Joey stomped around of the playroom I turned to Jack and asked "How does Joey feel now?" He answered, "Mad! No more Wii!" He followed it up with "I'll play it instead" and watched as Joey hit the red zone this time.

I guess his theory of mind is improving.

Similarly, we're trying help Jack understand there multiple ways to solve a problem or complete a task because this will hopefully help him to become a more flexible thinker. Brainstorming about different ways we can spend our afternoon, for example. Or, if time allows, I try to take a different route home to show Jack there's more than one path to travel.

Working Memory & Processing

Testing Jack's working memory, the evaluator read strings of random numbers with increasing length, and asked him to repeat it back. On the second part of the test, he had to listen to a string of numbers and repeat them back in reverse order. On both parts he scored well below age level, demonstrating that he's unable to hold information in his mind and work with it at the same time.

Improving Jack's focus and concentration will help increase his working memory and processing speed. Our psychologist suggested having Jack "warm up" with easier material at school before moving to more challenging work. Likewise, because his ability to focus is limited, it's helpful to reduce competitive demands so he can concentrate on one area at a time; if he needs to think creatively during a writing assignment, then he shouldn't have to worry so much about handwriting.

The goal is to get him to master one aspect of the overall project and then move him on to the other elements. At home, I try to zero in on one aspect of a chore, like having him make his bed neatly without rushing him to finish it quickly.

Auditory and Visual Complexity

Since Jack has trouble managing too much auditory noise at once, we've learned to give brief, concise directions like "Get milk please" or "Put shoes on". I have a tendency to over explain my instructions; before I might have told Jack something like "Could you please get me more milk out of the refrigerator? We need it for cereal." He would've stopped listening at "refrigerator". When I noticed he was tuning out, I'd start the whole dialogue over again, and take it even further: "You want cereal, don't you? Aren't you hungry? You need to eat to have a good day!" I'd be rewarded with a blank, empty stare.

Get milk. Please.

(Note: direct communication seems to work with all of my kids. They respond faster and understand instructions better. I guess I was just talking too much before.)

At school, we're working on increasing his tolerance for noise by modifying the time he spends in verbal activities like circle time and reading group. Throughout the winter, he read first at the table and then was excused for another activity while the rest of the students completed their portion. Over the course of several months his teacher increased his time with the group, and now he sits and listens for the majority of it.

Visually, we decided it was best to reduce the clutter in Jack's work spaces so he could focus and concentrate. Any kind of visual complexity can send him right into the red zone; whirling around the room with his fingers in his mouth.

Math worksheets are one of the biggest culprits. Throughout the fall I'd reach into his homework folder and my heart would sink if I saw a math sheet jumbled with numbers and problems because I knew I had a good half-hour battle ahead of me. The second Jack even glanced at the sheet he would burst into flames. "I can't do THAT! I'm not good at MATH!" I'd spend ten minutes just trying to convince him to sit at the counter with me and look it over.

After a few nights of red-zone hysteria we learned to use a piece of paper to cover up the problems so he only saw a few at a time. In school they do the same, and in some instances only have him complete a portion of the problems.

Jack feels better if he knows how much or how many of something he needs to finish before he starts to work. (And don't we all? I mean, aren't push-ups easier to do if we know how many we have?) If we warn him that he has to finish ten problems, he's much more likely to stay calm and regulated.

After a few months of incorporating all of these new strategies, I found myself at the same crossroad as when he was three. Can little games like "Waiter" really help Jack understand that others have thoughts and feelings too? Some days reminding Jack to jump on the trampoline seems pointless in the looming face of autism.

But that's life with a special needs kiddo. Every day you have to show up, stand up, and stretch without breaking.

Someone I'm With Has Autism

Excerpt

Community

When Jack was first diagnosed with autism, my inclination was to hold him close to me.

And although I have never once concealed his diagnosis from a single person, never hid his autism or kept it a secret, in many ways I positioned myself as his mediator. This was not exactly a conscious decision—since he was an infant I've had to translate, interpret, decode for him and for those around him; *he wants a cookie* and *the music is too loud* and *Jack wave good-bye wave you can do it wave.*

I guess you could say I was reluctant to release my little fish; to let him swim in the deeper waters beyond our house, because I was afraid of how people would react to him. Would the cashier in the Walgreens find him rude? Would the server in Bertucci's understand he's asking for milk and will the teachers in preschool remember to warn him about the fire drill?

I doubted our community.

I longed for Buffalo, where Jack was born and diagnosed and somewhat understood. We lived on a beautiful tree-lined street and we walked everywhere because there were sidewalks. There was an adorable bagel shop around the corner we used to go to for coffee on Saturday mornings.

It was a great community.

It's so easy to bandy that expression around, isn't it? *Oh, what a great community! We love the community!*

But what does community really mean? Technically, it means a neighborhood, a group of people. Decent schools and a low crime rate. You can find those things in a lot of places.

But the Buffalo community was more than that, and I can sum it up perfectly with my memory of an evening in November eight years ago.

Our oldest, Joey, was three years old. Jack was two, and Charlie just eight weeks. (Rose was a French Martini in the distant future, and Henry a gleam in the unreliable urologist's eye.)

Infant Charlie had an ear infection. For two nights he howled with the piercing pain, and the pediatrician had put him on an antibiotic that afternoon. For most of the evening he seemed listless, lethargic, and I remember him raising his tiny hands and sort of swiping at his eyes. I took him up for his bath and something about the way he moved and whined as I undressed him made me uneasy.

Holding him with just his diaper on, I walked downstairs and told Joe, "Something is wrong. He doesn't look right to me."

Sure enough, in the bright light of the living room I saw what I didn't notice in the dim light of the bathroom; his entire body was covered in hives. All I could think was that he looked like a pineapple.

"Call 911, he's having a reaction to the antibiotic," Joe commanded, taking Charlie into his arms.

Five minutes later the house was filled with burly ENT's; men wearing white shirts and navy pants and big, heavy work boots. One cradled Charlie in his arms in the corner of the dining room and said weird words like *EPI pen* and *anaphylactic* while I felt my own throat close with panic.

Two-year old Jack had just been diagnosed with autism, and he kept walking up to the ENT's and grabbing their hands, trying to lead them to the canister of cookies we kept in the kitchen.

After a moment it was decided that an ambulance ride to the emergency room was in order. I raced through the house grabbing clothes for the baby and a jacket for myself, while Joe scrambled to look up the babysitter's number so he could meet me at the hospital.

Cradling Charlie in my arms, I flung open the front door and blinked. On our front lawn stood nearly three dozen neighbors. In the dusky light they appeared motionless, until Mr. Simon—the attorney from down the street who walked his dog little Boots past our house every morning—stepped forward and broke the silence.

"What happened? What do you need?"

And all at once there was a tumble of words and hugs and hands on our shoulders. The ENT's strapped little Charlie to big stretcher and loaded him into the ambulance while people reassured us *it's going to be fine we'll stay with the kids you both go.*

That is what the community in Buffalo looked like; a group of neighbors waiting on the front lawn in the chilly November air, waiting to hear why the ambulance was there, if everyone was okay, if there was anything they could do.

Less than two years later, we moved to New Hampshire. And it was an adjustment.

There are no sidewalks. No cute bagel shops. The houses are more spread out, and I can go weeks without seeing my neighbors, especially in the winter. The community certainly felt different from the one we left in Buffalo.

But we settled in and got Jack situated at BEEP, the integrated preschool. We had our daughter, Rose, and accidentally had our last son, Henry. We joined Little League teams and karate and book clubs and poker groups. We went to church.

And before long, the community in Bedford began to bloom like the dogwoods in spring; slow to blossom but brilliant in color.

But despite a close circle of friends and play dates and school activities, nothing quite captured the feeling I experienced that evening in Buffalo; the feeling we were held together by more than just carpooling and coat drives, potluck dinners and monthly card games.

Until last spring.

We had been living here for six years. Jack had just been diagnosed with amblyopia, also known as lazy eye. Basically, his right side had been doing all the work for his idle I-want-to-sit-on-the-couch-and-eat-potato-chips-all day left, until his left eye lost enough sight to be declared legally blind.

Joe and I were reeling; guilty and frustrated that we'd never detected it or investigated his quirky habit of reading out of the right eye more seriously. Combined with his autism, it seemed like just one more challenge Jack would have to compensate for, one more thing to overcome.

Someone else was also reeling: Jack. The pediatric opthamologist said he needed to wear a patch over his right eye for two hours a day to strengthen the right, and she also prescribed glasses.

Oh, the glasses. For six hours, this boy raged and seethed and shrieked and cried over those glasses. And that was before we even ordered them or picked out the frames.

That evening—the evening of the six-hour tantrum about glasses—we put Jack to bed, and when I went in to kiss him goodnight, he pulled his weighted blanket up to his chin and chanted tearfully, "No glasses. No glasses. I just want to be normal. Normal."

I wandered back downstairs, feeling despondent and hopeless like I always do after one of Jack's marathon tantrums. I e-mailed his teacher to update her on the appointment and explained his resistance to glasses.

Anxious and restless, I hopped on Facebook, and I saw this message she posted, minutes after reading my e-mail:

"Riddle Brook friends......please wear glasses tomorrow if you don't regularly do so. It is a for a great kiddo who might need some encouragement as he faces a new zig in his zag:)"

And my heart soared.

By 6:15 the next morning, Jack was standing over my bed chanting, "No glasses. No glasses. I will not wear **GLASSES**!"

As he munched his Cheerios I told him I thought the teachers had something funny planned, something to cheer him up, but he just griped, "I am not going to school today **EITHER**." Grumpily he trundled to the bus and stomped up the stairs without a look back.

All day, as I ran to Hannaford's and picked up dry cleaning and bought stamps, I thought about Jack, worried he was lost to his inner world of anguish over eyewear. But just as the bus pulled up, I checked e-mail on my phone and saw this picture from his teacher.

Jack got off the bus and slumped into his seat in the van. "Okay, okay, okay," he said, holding his tattered red backpack on his lap, "I will try my best. With these glasses." And off we went to the optometrist's, where he picked out an electric blue pair of spectacles without any prompting at all.

It took a group of teachers dusting off their glasses to help my son on the spectrum find his way through a new transition, to show him they understand him, they embrace him, they accept him and his autism.

They helped my unusual boy feel normal, even if just for a little while.

This is community.

Now, when I see the cashier in Walgreens smile and hand Jack his bag, when I look at the picture of teachers who wear glasses, I know I am ready to let Jack go, out into the cool, deep pond and into the wide, wavy blue world beyond.

Estrangement: An Essay

from www.carriecariello.com

The room is quiet now. The lights are low.

You are asleep, a white blanket pulled up close, your hands limp at your sides.

A few hours earlier, the doctor ticked off all the betrayals of your body while a machine pumped air through your lungs.

Advanced COPD.

Pulmonary embolism.

Heart failure.

Now, the air is still. The breath-machine has been removed. The tube is gone from your throat.

Beneath the covers, you are small. Diminutive, even. It is a stark contrast to your presence throughout my childhood. Although petite in stature, you always loomed large.

Memories compete for space in my mind—a slideshow of color and light.

Jumping through waves on the beach at Cape Cod.

Rollercoaster rides at the county fair, the Cosby Show on Thursday nights, your face in the audience as I played the flute.

Sharing a brownie sundae at TGI Fridays during one of our last meals out together.

Yet each slide is punctuated with chaos, like too many exclamation points in a paragraph.

A full-size aquarium smashed in pieces.

Screaming matches on the front lawn.

Long periods of silence following destruction.

For as long as I can remember, proverbial eggshells littered the carpet in our house. We tread carefully.

Estranged. That is what we are. A word with a bad consonant-to-vowel ratio.

It's not something I talk about often.

After all, what kind of daughter doesn't speak to her mother?

How bad, how strained, how tense could it be that you can't find a shred of goodness between one another?

We couldn't.

Now, here in this room, I consider the word carefully.

Estranged.

If you are prone to numbers, which I am not, I'd say we've seen each other a dozen times in as many years.

 Still, every now and again, you surface into the periphery of my mind.

A book we both enjoyed, sitting still and dusty on the shelf.

A song by your beloved Rick Astley on the radio.

The smell of cigarettes mingled with strong coffee.

Your green eyes reflected in my oldest son.

Do I wish I could change it?

Not necessarily.

I wish I had savored the softer moments between us, perhaps. I wish I held on more tightly to the smiles over chocolate and whipped cream —the salty waves beneath a cloudless sky.

I wish mental health was more than a concealed whisper amongst your generation. I wish medication and therapy had been a part of the conversation.

Who am I without you, my invisible, perpetual antagonist?

For it is against your emotional tide that I swim, hoping I didn't inherit the same capacity for rip tides.

When my maternal ghosts haunt me, and I hear a familiar shrillness in my own voice, I remind myself.

I have built something new.

I have built something different.

Always, you wanted me to choose.

Father.

Stepmother.

Eventually, husband.

To love another was to shortchange you. Attachment was a limited resource. I guess you could say I wasn't always good with choices.

It's not as though you had it easy. Divorce. Three children under eight. Two jobs. Night school.

External forces combined with your inner turmoil to create a force field of rage, paranoia, and deep-seated anxiety. You waged your private war upon everyone you encountered.

Still, I cling to the idea that all is not gone. All is not lost.

A love of books, a sense of fearlessness, the appreciation for a good joke.

This is what you give me. This is your legacy. In turn, I will pass it to my own children. The books, the courage, the laughter.

The doctor says it could be a week. Schedules are made for coverage in the hospital because, like anything else, death is prosaic. It is practical. It demands organization.

Now, visiting hours are over. I make my way through the labyrinth of hallways and elevators. Outside, the summer sun is an orange ball of fire over my head. As I pull out of the lot, I turn six words around in my mind.

Over and over we said them, a mother-daughter circle of apology, of forgiveness, of redemption.

We did the best we could.

Rest now. May your heart know peace at last.